THE ROYAL CRESCENT
— BOOK OF —
BATH

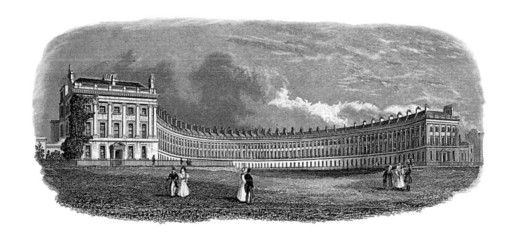

THE ROYAL CRESCENT
— BOOK OF —
BATH

JAMES CRATHORNE

COLLINS & BROWN

First published in Great Britain in 1998 by
Collins & Brown Limited
London House, Great Eastern Wharf
Parkgate Road, London SW11 4NQ

1 3 5 7 9 8 6 4 2

A CIP record for this book is available from the British Library.

ISBN 1 85585 498 8 (hardback edition)

Conceived, edited and designed by
Collins & Brown Limited

Editorial Director Colin Ziegler
Art Director Roger Bristow
Project Editor Elizabeth Drury
Researcher Susanna Johnston
Picture Researcher Philippa Lewis
Designer Claire Graham

Reproduction by Hong Kong Graphics and Printing
Printed and bound in Singapore by CS Graphics

CONTENTS

INTRODUCTION

Bath is the most elegant and enchanting of cities, an architectural spectacle with a history that involves a procession of colourful characters. This is the story of Bath, the place and the people.

In the beginning it was a belief in the healing powers of the spring waters that drew people to this corner of the west of England. Situated beside the River Avon, Bath is surrounded by hills, and from these hills came the honey-coloured stone of which the city at every stage in its long history was built. The colour of the stone gives Bath an air of placid contentment, a sense that the buildings have every right to be there.

Celtic origins centred around a sacred spring. When the territory was occupied by the Romans, they constructed baths fed by the spring and a temple dedicated to Sulis Minerva, combining the two cultures – Celtic and Roman. In the Middle Ages an abbey was founded, and a town grew up around it. Doctors and quacks set up in lucrative practice, and visitors came from far and wide to drink and bathe in the waters. The presence of royalty attracted people of fashion. In 1724 Daniel Defoe was to write:

> in former times this was a resort hither for cripples;
> and we see the crutches hang up at the several baths,
> as the thank-offerings of those who have come hither
> lame, and gone away cured. But now we may say it is

LEFT *The hall of No. 16 Royal Crescent, The Royal Crescent hotel. The black and white chequered floor and the hall chairs are characteristic of the Georgian period. The halberds on either side of the door were used in the eighteenth century for ceremonial purposes.*

ABOVE *Royal Crescent in 1788, a detail from a watercolour by Thomas Malton the Younger. John Wood the Younger's architectural masterpiece was begun in 1767, and was the first and most famous of the Georgian crescents. It was widely copied elsewhere in Britain.*

the resort of the sound, rather than the sick; the bathing is made more a sport and diversion, than a physical prescription for health; and the town is taken up in raffling, gaming, visiting, and in a word, all sorts of gallantry and levity.

The Georgian city owed its development and popularity to a triumvirate. Beau Nash, professional gambler and *bon viveur*, was the undisputed 'King of Bath'. As Master of Ceremonies, he introduced a code of courtly conduct and dress, and set the scene for the fashionable – and the would-be fashionable – to mingle and pursue a round of pleasure and entertainment. Ralph Allen made a fortune through his reforms of the postal system and with the proceeds bought the local stone quarry at Combe Down. He devised ingenious and economical working methods at the quarry, and provided the stone that was used by the architect John Wood –

and later by his son of the same name – to make Bath one of the wonders of Europe.

The architectural character of Bath derives from the grandeur of its plan and from the classical detail of the eighteenth-century buildings, designed – or in some senses inspired – by the Woods. Royal Crescent is, perhaps, the supreme example of Georgian elegance, and occupying the centre of the Crescent is one of the world's finest hotels, where the spirit of the eighteenth century has been splendidly recreated. The architectural importance of Bath was recognized when in 1987 it was designated a World Heritage Site; the buildings are now treated with the care and respect that will ensure their survival.

The Assembly Rooms and the Pump Room, the Circus, the rows of houses, crescents and squares, are full of memories of the fashionable and famous people who came to Bath in its heyday: Samuel Pepys and Celia Fiennes, the 'Grand Old' Duke of York and his duchess, Richard Brinsley Sheridan, Lord Chesterfield, the original bluestocking Mrs Elizabeth Montagu, the pretentious Lady Miller, Thomas Gainsborough and Jane Austen. Some of them, and the novelists Tobias Smollett and Charles Dickens as well, have given us descriptions – both truthful and elaborated, and frequently humorous – of the visitors and of how days were passed in this place of resort: in taking the cure, dancing and playing at cards, shopping for bonnets and buckles, parading in fine clothes, appearing in church or chapel, making assignations and exchanging *billets-doux*.

However, the story of Bath is not only about the past. It is today a vibrant city, where music and the theatre provide regular entertainment. There is boating on the river and ballooning, streets of fine shops as well as buildings and galleries to visit. The future holds the promise of a rejuvenated spa city, with up-to-date facilities for bathing and obtaining the benefits from the thermal waters. After all, it is to the springs that rise in the heart of the city that Bath owes its beginnings.

IN THE MISTS
OF TIME

THE DISCOVERY OF FLINT arrowheads reveals that Stone Age hunters roamed the area around Bath 5,000 years before the Romans arrived. During excavation of the King's Bath spring in the twentieth century, eighteen Celtic coins were found, some 2,000 years after their original owners had cast them into the steamy, bubbling, rust-coloured water as an offering to Sulis, goddess of the spring, worshipped for her powers of healing.

The hot springs in Bath are unique in the British Isles. For at least 10,000 years three springs have emerged from the clay within a quarter of a mile (400 metres) of each other. The temperature of the hottest spring is 49°C (119°F); it became known as the Hetling Spring, supplying the medieval and the Georgian Hot Bath. The largest spring, bubbling up at 46°C (115°F) and at 250,000 gallons (1,136,500 litres) a day, was for the Romans the Sacred Spring; the water was channelled into their Great Bath, later to become the King's Bath. The coolest spring rises at 40°C (116°F) and would feed the Cross Bath.

Six thousand years after falling as rain on the Mendip hills, the water is forced up through fissures in the limestone crust. It then lies beneath the clay before rising through the fault that lies below Bath, hot and rich in forty-three different minerals, including calcium and sodium, and iron, which gives the water its distinctive colour and flavour.

The springs were a source of wonder to all who saw them, and it is not surprising that they should have been viewed as a sacred place by both the prehistoric inhabitants of the area and the

BELOW *The façade of the Temple of Minerva, as reconstructed from fragments of carved stone, a plate from* Reliquiae Britannico-Romanae, *1813, by Samuel Lysons.*

Roman invaders after them. Under the command of Aulus Plautius, the invasionary force landed in Britain in AD 43, during the rule of the Emperor Claudius. They had arrived at the limit of the known world. A frontier of the Empire had to be established and the local tribes suppressed. Before he returned to Rome in AD 47, Aulus Plautius had established a line of garrisons down which a road, the Fosse Way, would later be built. This stretched from Exeter east to the Humber and crossed the Avon at a point where was to be founded the first city of Bath: Aquae Sulis, the Waters of Sulis.

ROMAN BATH

Attendance at public baths was an important part of daily life to the Romans, and it is likely that the occupying soldiers bathed in the hot springs and that the authorities observed the power of the local deity. By the end of the first century AD the Romans had created on the sacred Celtic site a grand range of buildings: a temple, an inner and an outer precinct, and baths. The temple was dedicated to Sulis Minerva, a combination of the Celtic Sulis and the Roman goddess of healing, Minerva.

ABOVE LEFT *The central feature of the temple pediment, the massive Gorgon's head, carved by the Romans and incorporating Celtic imagery. The head was discovered in 1790, when the architect Thomas Baldwin set his men to dig the foundations of the new Pump Room.*

ABOVE *One of the precious gold coins thrown into the Sacred Spring as an offering to the goddess Sulis Minerva. The coin has been calculated as representing two months' salary for a fairly high-ranking official. It was part of the treasure trove found during the excavation of the spring in 1979–80.*

This conflation of two gods was common practice for the Romans in outlying provinces, and was a way of placating local sensibilities. Here it was powerfully expressed in the intensely dramatic Gorgon's head carved on the pediment, which was supported on four massive Corinthian columns at the entrance of the temple. The Gorgon was associated with the power of Minerva, who in classical mythology turned the snake-haired Medusa, chief of the Gorgons, to stone. The Gorgon mask at Bath is male, not female, a fierce Celtic head with flowing moustaches and a furrowed brow.

The pediment is incomplete, but fragments other than the Gorgon survive to give an idea of how it looked originally. They include a wreath of British oak leaves, and an owl and a helmet – both symbols of Minerva. The intertwined snakes among the radiating hair may be interpreted as symbols of healing.

The inner temple precinct was enclosed by a colonnade. In front of the temple stood the sacrificial altar and beside it the Sacred Spring. The spring was originally open to the sky but later covered with a cavernous barrel vault. This would have made it appear as a dark and mysterious grotto, with light filtering in through a large Diocletian window built high at one end. Supplications were made to the goddess by throwing offerings into the pool. These were objects valued by the worshippers and considered worthy of the goddess: gold, silver, bronze and brass coins, jewellery, engraved gemstones, and pewter and silver vessels, many of which were inscribed with the name Sulis Minerva.

The concerns of Roman visitors during the first three hundred years of the millennium are vividly brought to life by reading the 'curses' that were also thrown into the spring. These little folds and rolls of pewter and lead are scratched with messages for the goddess: 'Dodimedis has lost two gloves. He asks that the person who has stolen them should lose his mind and his eyes in the temple where she appoints'; 'To Minerva the goddess Sulis I have given the thief who stole my hooded cloak, whether slave or free, man or woman. He is not to buy back this gift unless with his own blood'; 'May he who has stolen Vilbia from me become as liquid as water.'

BELOW *One of the Roman lead 'curses' found in the Sacred Spring. The complainant writes of a lost possession. He wishes that the thief 'become as liquid as water' and offers the goddess a list of possible malefactors.*

LEFT *Five fragments of a pediment with a carved representation of the goddess Luna, found in 1790. The Roman deity is identified by the crescent moon behind her head and the whip in her left hand, which she used to drive her chariot across the night sky.*

Ornamenting the façades of the temple precincts were depictions of the sun god Sol, the Four Seasons, the moon goddess Luna and Diana, goddess of hunting. Among these large architectural pieces were small altars erected as memorials: 'To the goddess Sulis Minerva and to the deities of the two emperors, Gaius Curatius Saturninus, centurion of the 2nd Legion Augusta, willingly and deservedly fulfilled his vow for himself and his kindred.'

Tombstones from cemeteries on the roads leading into the city give a picture of the inhabitants of Roman Bath in precisely the same manner as the eighteenth-century monuments in the Abbey do for a later period: 'Lucius Vitellius Tancinus, a tribesman of Caurium in Spain, trooper of the cavalry regiment of Vettones with twenty-six years of service to the Roman Empire'; 'Julius Vitalis, a Belgic tribesman, armourer of the Twentieth Legion with nine years of service.'

The fame of the hot springs at Bath spread throughout the ancient world: Ptolemy of Alexandria listed the *Aquae Calidae* (Hot Waters) in his *Geography* of the second century AD. The

Roman writer Solinus a century later described the hot springs, though not at first hand, as being:

> furnished luxuriously for human use . . . over these springs Minerva presides and in her temple the perpetual fire never whitens to ash, but as the flame fades, turns into rocky lumps.

This last is probably a reference to cinders from the Somerset coal discovered and used as fuel by the Romans. The stone they quarried from the hills around Bath, and the lead for the pipes and lining of the Great Bath, came from mines in the Mendip hills. Clay for the Roman tile bricks, limestone for mortar and wood for construction were all to be found locally.

By the third century the Romans had built extensively in the area that lay outside the temple precincts, providing all manner of luxurious facilities. The Great Bath to the south was fed directly by a lead pipe from the reservoir around the Sacred Spring, and it was surrounded by ambulatories floored with smooth limestone slabs. There was the cold bath, the *frigidarium*, a warm room, or *tepidarium*, a hot room, the *caldarium*, and the *laconicum*, which was very hot indeed.

After the Roman Empire disintegrated, at the end of the fourth century, all the careful systems of drainage and water control fell into disrepair; gradually the water level rose, and the buildings were slowly engulfed in mud and virtually forgotten. Scholars in later centuries would make references to the past. Dr Thomas Guidott wrote in his *Briefe Discourse* of 1659:

> There is a tradition that there was formerly a temple dedicated to Minerva, where now the Church of St Peter and St Paul, commonly called the Abbey Church, stands.

One of the curses found in the mud has an inscription that begins, 'Whether pagan or Christian, whosoever, whether man or woman, whether boy or girl, whether slave or free, has stolen from me . . .' The mention of Christianity provides a pointer to the future of Bath, and to the next great building phase in the history of the city.

ABOVE *Tombstones of Roman soldiers, illustrated by Samuel Lysons. The one at the top commemorates a Spaniard, Lucius Vitellius Tancinus, who gave twenty-six years' service as a trooper in a cavalry regiment. The lower stone was erected to the memory of Julius Vitalis, an armourer of the Twentieth Legion who died aged twenty-nine.*

ABOVE *Tombstones of Roman citizens have been unearthed in various parts of the city. This fragment shows a man holding a staff in one hand and a scroll in the other, with a purse hanging from his belt.*

ABOVE Prince Bladud Contemplating the Medicinal Virtues of Bath Waters by Observing their Effect on Swine, *a pen, ink and wash drawing by Benjamin West, inscribed 'Bath Sep 20 1807'.*

In the eighth century there was a monastic community in Bath, dedicated to St Peter, and a fine Anglo-Saxon abbey, which probably incorporated stone from the Roman ruins. It was through the monastic tradition of writing that knowledge of the curative powers of the spring at the temple was passed down. The Welsh cleric Geoffrey of Monmouth compiled in the mid-twelfth century a *Historia Britonum*, which chronicles the descent of British princes from Roman times, and in so doing he recounted much

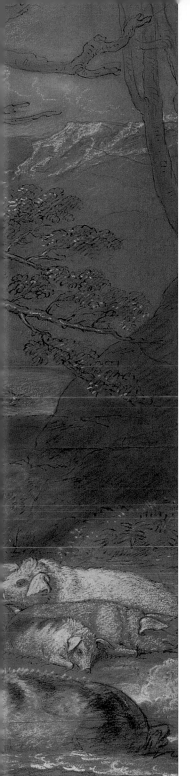

of the legend of King Arthur. He also described the legend of King Bladud, whom he credited with the building of Bath and the hot baths.

KING BLADUD

The legendary Bladud was the son of King Lud Hudibras, grandson of King Brut (and father of King Lear). He was banished from his father's court when he contracted leprosy and took up the life of a swineherd. His pigs, too, became leprous. Taken by Bladud to feed on the acorns in the woods of the Avon valley, the pigs discovered the delights of wallowing in the warm oozy mud and water of the hot springs. Miraculously, they were cured of their leprosy. Bladud followed his pigs' example, and was also cured. Restored to society, he went to Athens and studied magic with Zoroaster, and philosophy and astronomy with Pythagoras. There he became known as Abaris, the Northern Sage. He returned after eleven years to take up the throne of Albion and build his capital, Bath, and to found a university for British Druids.

ABOVE *Head of the carved and painted stone figure of the legendary Bladud, who for centuries was believed to have founded Bath after his leprosy had been cured by bathing in the mineral waters.*

The Bladud legend persisted, and in the eighteenth century there were at least three statues commemorating the king. Two survive: one of medieval origin, which has been in the King's Bath since the 1600s, and an eighteenth-century relief in the Cross Bath, showing him as Abaris the Sage. At the opening of the first Pump Room in 1706 a song was sung that had been specially composed in honour of Bladud:

Great Bladud, born a sov'reign prince,
But from the court was banished thence
His dire disease to shun;
The Muses do his fame record,
That when the Bath his health restor'd,
Great Bladud did return.
This royal Prince of royal race,
The founder of this happy place,
Where beauty holds her reign;
To Bladud's mem'ry let us join,
And crown the glass from springs divine,
His glory to maintain.

The song continues in the same vein for a further three verses and ends on a bathetic note with Bladud's death, when his attempt to fly with 'artful wings' failed.

It was only in the early nineteenth century that historians such as John Britton, in his *History and Antiquities of the Abbey Church at Bath*, could dismiss the story as 'among the wildest fictions of an uncivilized age'; indeed, he mounted an attack on the architect John Wood who had repeated the story in his *Essay towards a Description of Bath* of 1742–3. 'We cannot but wonder,' wrote Britton, 'at the credulity of those whose education and station in life ought to keep them far above giving credence to vague and popular traditions, when unsupported by historical testimony.' A genuine English king, Edgar, was crowned at Bath on Whit Sunday 973.

THE MEDIEVAL AND TUDOR CITY

Gradually new buildings put up by the next wave of invaders, the Normans, overlaid the Roman ruins. John de Villula of Tours, chaplain and physician to William Rufus, after his elevation to

ABOVE A scene in the Cross Bath by Samuel Hieronymous Grimm: an attendant sweeps under the stone image of Bladud as Abaris. The original design for the figure was by the painter William Hoare. Grimm's drawing was done in 1789, just after the bath had been rebuilt by Thomas Baldwin.

Bishop of Wells in 1088, constructed a splendid monastic infirmary over the temple precincts and a Romanesque abbey church on the site of the Saxon abbey. The twelfth century saw also the building of a bishop's palace, a cloister and dormitories. A new bath (the one that later became known as the King's Bath) was built re-using the old Roman walls of the Great Bath. The baths came under the bishop's jurisdiction, and he diverted some of the water into the Priory for two other baths, one of which was for his private enjoyment. The town remained a centre of healing, and a twelfth-century manuscript relates:

> sick persons from all over England go there to bathe in the healing waters, as well as the healthy who go to see the wonderful outpourings of water and bathe in them.

By the fifteenth century the religious community was in some disarray: the number of monks had dwindled to eighteen, and there was constant bickering over whether Bath or Wells (which had been added to the diocese in 1091) held supremacy. Henry VIII went so far as to sack Bishop Hadrian de Castella, who was frequently in Italy and living a life of intrigue at the court of the

BELOW *Bath Abbey from the north-east, with the Orange Grove in the foreground. It is one of a series of prints after John Claude Nattes, published in 1806, and shows the turrets in their original form, before the nineteenth-century addition of pinnacles.*

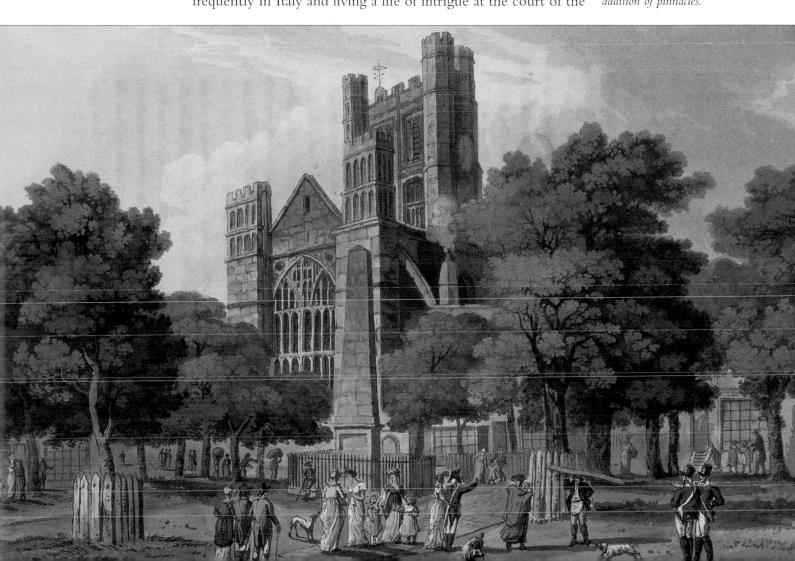

ABOVE *Detail of the west front of Bath Abbey showing the angels climbing up and down the ladder to heaven, inspired by the dream Bishop Oliver King had in 1499. The softness of the Bath stone means that much of the carving has had to be restored.*

Borgia pope instead of ministering to his flock in the west of England. The monks who remained expended their income on 'pleasurable indulgences' rather than on the upkeep of the abbey, which was reduced to a derelict state.

In 1499 Bishop Oliver King resolved to rebuild the church after reportedly having a dream while on a visit to the city. Sir John Harington later wrote that the bishop:

> lying at Bathe, and musing or meditating
> one night late, after his devotions and prayers
> for the prosperity of Henry VIIth and his
> children . . . to which King he was principal
> Secretary . . . saw, or supposed he saw, a vision
> of the Holy Trynitie, with angells ascending and
> descending by a ladder, neer to the foote of
> which there was a fayre Olive tree, supporting a
> crown, and a voyce that said – 'Let an OLIVE
> establish the *Crowne*, and let a KING restore
> the *Church*'. Of this dreame, or vision, he took
> exceeding great comfort, and told it divers of
> his friends, applying it to the King his master in
> parte, and some part to himselfe. To his master
> because the *Olive* being the emblem or hieroglifick of peace
> and plentie, seemed to him to allude to King Henry VIIth,
> who was worthely counted the wisest and most peaceable
> King in all Europe of that age. To himself (for the wisest
> will flatter themselves sometime) because he was not only
> a chiefe councellor to this King, and had bene his
> ambassador to conclude the most honourable peace
> with Charles the 8 . . . but also he carried both the *Olive*
> and the *King* in his own name.

Whether a vision or a dream, this type of word-play was beloved by the educated in the Middle Ages, and it is the source for the sculpture on the west façade of the present Abbey.

Bishop King ordered that a major proportion of the revenue from the Priory should be spent on rebuilding the church and gave Prior Birde responsibility for supervising the work. Not to be outdone in the search for lasting glory, Prior Birde built a chapel for himself decorated with his rebus, a 'W' for William and a bird. The King's own masons, William and Robert Vertue, were

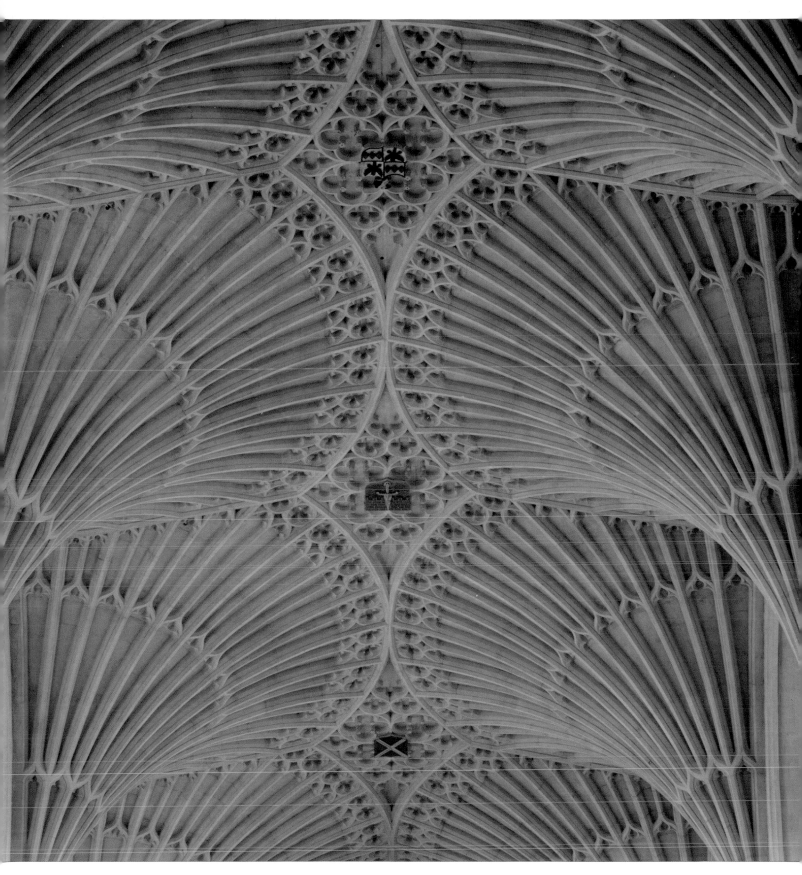

ABOVE *The earliest part of the stone fan-vaulted roof of the Abbey was built by the masons William and Robert Vertue, who assured Bishop Oliver that there would be 'none so goodely neither in England nor in France.' The fan-vaulting was not completed until 1869.*

employed on the building, and there arose from the ruins of the old Norman church one of the last churches in England to be built in the Perpendicular Gothic style. Disastrously, it was unfinished at the time of the dissolution of the monasteries in the late 1530s. The lead intended for the roof was stolen, the bells melted, stone and glass moved away, and once again it was badly neglected. Harington described how the following words were scrawled on the walls:

> O Church! I waile thy wofull plight
> Whom King nor Card'nall, nor Clerke nor Knight
> Have yet restor'd to auncient right.

Perhaps Harington, who was Elizabeth I's godson, told her of these lines and of the plight of the Abbey, for in 1574 the Queen appealed for funds to save the building. As a result, a group of local worthies, including Harington, Peter Chapman, a wool merchant, and Thomas Bellott, steward to Lord Burghley, came forward to finish the roof and the glazing.

In 1590 Queen Elizabeth granted the city a new charter, which removed the Bath waters from the jurisdiction of the Abbey and made the 'body of citizens, and their successors, perpetual guardians of the city and hot waters'. The following year, when the Queen visited Bath while staying with Harington, the stench

BELOW LEFT Victorian studies of ornamental details from the ceiling of Prior Birde's chantry chapel in the Abbey, begun in 1515, showing his initials and his rebus. The watercolours record the work of the architect E. Davis, who restored the chapel in the nineteenth century.

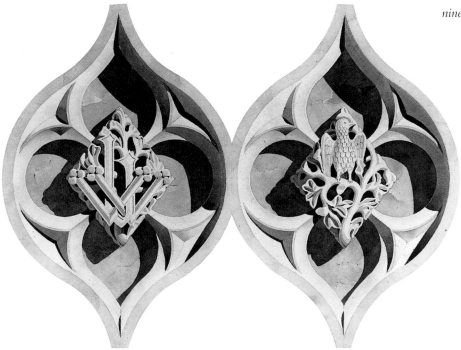

from the open sewers was such that she gained an unfavourable impression of the place. Her host, writing in 1591 to Lord Burghley, complained that the city, and particularly the Abbey church, were fast decaying, and said of the pitiful lack of adequate sewers:

> for a town so plentifully served of water, in a country
> so well provided of stone, in a place resorted unto so
> greatly, methink [it] seemeth an unworthy and
> dishonourable thing.

He had no doubt, however, that if the revenues were properly applied, the ruined church would become a 'reverent church' and this 'unsavoury' town would become 'a most sweet town'.

TAKING
THE CURE

FOLLOWING ELIZABETH I's visit, other persons of distinction came to Bath. They were drawn by the reputation of the waters for curing medical disorders and restoring health. Claims of the waters' efficacy were supported by the influential Dr William Turner, who published in 1562 *A Book of the Natures and Properties as well as of the Bathes in England*:

> Bathes of brimstone soften the sinews, suage the pain that a
> man hath in defying the going often unto the stool and
> when he cometh thither can do little or nothing. They
> scour and cleanse the skin wherefore they are good for the
> white and black morphews [pimples], for leprosy and scabs,
> scurf, for old sores and blotches and for the falling of
> humours into joints.

It was for the alleviation of rheumatism, paralysis (probably caused by lead poisoning) and gout that the waters became especially renowned; and for female ailments as well. Two royal spouses, Catherine of Braganza, wife of Charles II, and Mary of Modena, consort of James II, both came to test 'the wonder-working powers of the Bath Waters in cases of barrenness'. In the latter instance the Queen conceived: the child, James Stuart, was to become known as the 'Old Pretender'.

DOCTORS OF THE SEVENTEENTH CENTURY

Dr Robert Peirce in his memoirs of Bath published in 1697 asserted that the waters had been drunk 'time out of mind' for two purposes:

ABOVE *Frontispiece to one of Dr Guidott's publications extolling the benefits to be derived from the Bath waters. He commented, 'Empiricks and juggling medicasters do so much abound here that 'tis almost as hard now to meet with a regular and accomplished physician as it was in former times for Diogenes to meet an honest man.'*

to quench thirst, and to keep Soluble. They that used the Baths for cold distempers, as palsies and withered limbs, &c. were forced to continue long in them, and to sweat much, which rendered them both thirsty and costive; to both which the Waters were a known remedy; for it had been long observed, and is now very well known, that a draught or two of the Bath Water quencheth thirst better and more effectual than double the quantity of beer or ale, or any other usual beverage; and when by spending the moisture in long and much sweating, the bowels were heated, and dried, and rendered constipate, a large draught of this water, with a little common salt, would give a stool or two.

Peirce treated the Duke of Lauderdale 'for more than ordinary corpulency and scorbutical distempers' and Sir Alexander Frayser, physician to Charles II and Catherine of Braganza, 'for an old cough and cathetick habit of body':

both went off much advantaged; the Duke losing a large span of his girth; and Sir Alexander getting more breath, and a fresh and better-coloured countenance; being pale, and sallow, and black under the eyes, when he first came down.

Doctors at this time were 'prescribing to their unhappy patients potations sufficiently large to have cleansed the Augean stable'. Dr Guidott recommended that those:

a size stronger in constitution, larger bodies, and more violent distempers, may take a *pottle* at first in an hour's time, and so rise up by steps . . . to a *gallon*, which I judge sufficient for the middle sort: and those that are of the larger size, and thought fit to bear the greatest proportion, may begin with *five pints*, and come up to *ten*.

Dr Jorden, a physician held in high regard, would not encourage the waters' internal use, 'as they could not be procured clean enough for drinking'. On the subject of immersion in the waters, he was of the opinion that it was unwise to eat or drink after bathing until a sleep had been taken, and a walk. If walking was not practicable, the patient must 'be lightly rubbed and if not able to be rubbed take a suppository of beetroot with a little salt, or honey, fleur de luce, or salt bacon, or white soap'.

BELOW *Frontispiece to Dr Jorden's work on the waters of Bath published in 1633. According to Dr Guidott, Jorden 'had the applause of the learned, respect from the rich, the prayers of the poor, and the love of all'.*

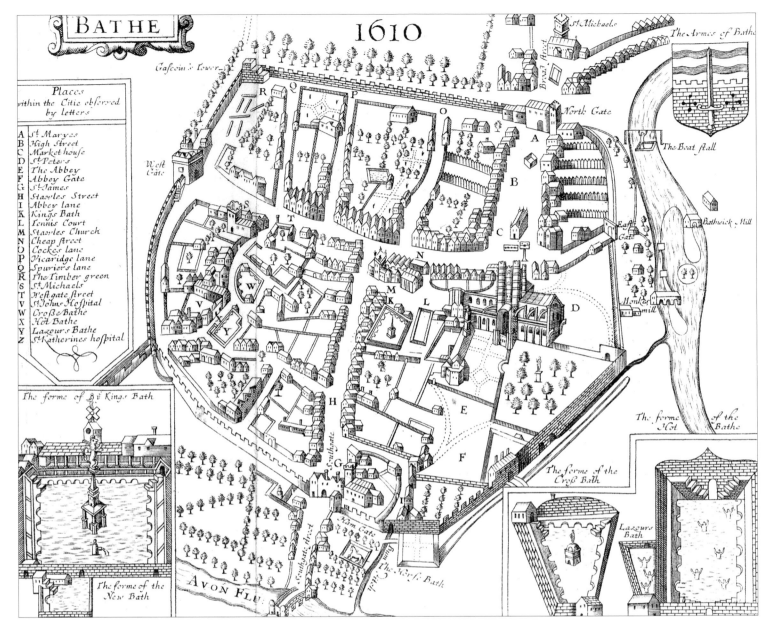

Places
within the Citie observed
by letters

A St Maryes
B High Street
C Market house
D St Peters
E The Abbey
F Abbey Gate
G St James
H Stawles Street
I Abbey lane
K Kings Bath
L Tennis Court
M Stawles Church
N Cheap Street
O Cockes lane
P Vicaridge lane
Q Spurlers lane
R The Timber green
S St Michaels
T Weftgate street
V St Johns Hospital
W Crosse Bathe
X Hot Bathe
Y Lazeurs Bathe
Z St Katherines hospital

The forme of y Kings Bath

The forme of the New Bath

The forme of the Cross Bath

Lazeurs Bath

VISITORS' DESCRIPTIONS OF THE BATHS

In the early seventeenth century, according to John Wood (writing his *Description of Bath* more than a hundred years later and with the intention of demonstrating the improvements he had brought to the city):

> The baths were like so many bear-gardens, and modesty
> was entirely shut out of them; people of both sexes bathing
> by day and night naked; and dogs, cats, and pigs, even
> human creatures, were hurl'd over the rails into the water,
> while people were bathing in it.

In 1646 the Corporation of Bath decreed, again in Wood's words:

> that no man or woman should go into any one of the
> baths, by day or night, without a decent covering on their

ABOVE *Map of Bath engraved by John Speed and published in his* Theatre of the Empire of Great Britain *in 1611–12. The Abbey dominates the city, though the nave has no roof. The monastery, which included the Abbey and the King's Bath, was dissolved in 1539, which brought work to a halt. Around the map are vignettes of the baths.*

bodies, under the like penalty of three shillings and fourpence. That no person shall presume to cast or throw any dog, bitch, or other live beast into any of the said baths under the like penalty of three shillings and fourpence. That no person shall thrust, cast, or throw into any of the said Baths, with his or her clothes on, under penalty of six shillings and eightpence. That no person or persons shall disorderly or uncivilly demean themselves in the said Baths, on pain of forfeiting five shillings.

By the time Celia Fiennes visited the city towards the end of the century there was 'a serjeant belonging to the baths that all the bathing tyme walks in galleryes and takes notice order is observed and punishes the rude'.

Samuel Pepys on a visit to Bath in 1668 had risen at the unusually early hour of four in the morning to avoid the throng in the Cross Bath and had found 'the manner pretty enough':

Good conversation among them that are acquainted here, and stay together. Strange to see how hot the water is; and in some places, though this is the most temperate bath, the springs so hot as the feet not able to endure. But strange to see, when women and men herein, that live all the season in these waters, that cannot but be parboiled, and looke like the creatures of the bath!

ABOVE *A detail of the 'kitchen' in the King's Bath, from an engraving by John Fayram of 1738/9. The kitchen was where the water bubbled up into the bath and was at its hottest; sitting there was likened to being in a hot kitchen. The crutches cast aside by cripples who had been cured by bathing in the waters can be seen attached to the cupola.*

He stayed for more than two hours in the water before being wrapped in a sheet and carried home in a chair. Back at his lodgings he lay sweating for an hour as part of the treatment.

Also in his diary Pepys wrote, 'methinks it cannot be clean to go so many bodies together in the same water', and misgivings about the cleanliness of the baths were not uncommon even though they were emptied through sluices once, or even twice, each day and filled up again by the spring. Celia Fiennes saw for herself the water bubbling up through the gravel at the bottom of the baths. She drank the waters at the pump and found it

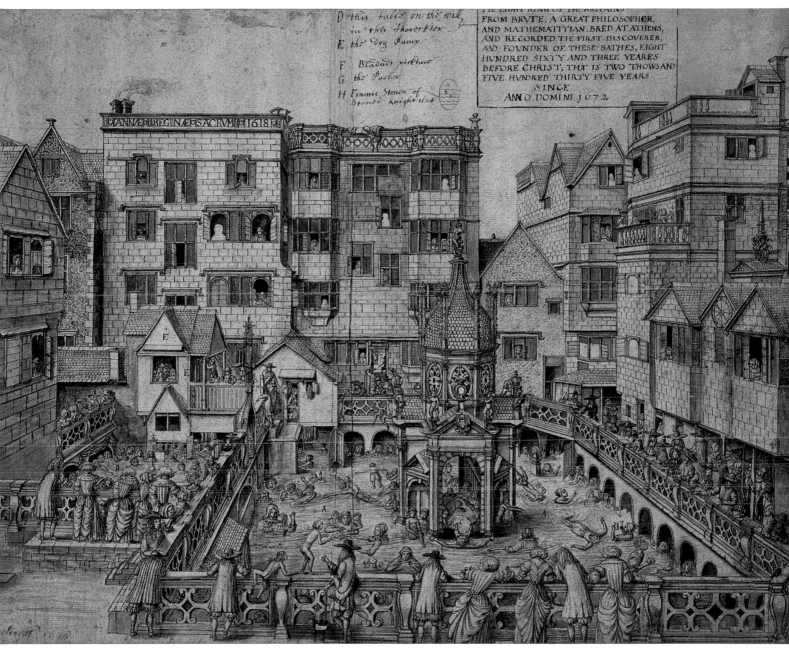

The following labels appear within the drawing:

D *this table on the wall in this threerellox*
E *the dry Pump*
F *Bladuds virtues*
G *the Pastox*
H *Franris Stoner of Stoner Knight 1624*

[...] *THE EIGHT KING OF THE BRITAINS FROM BRVTE, A GREAT PHILOSOPHER, AND MATHEMATITIAN: BRED AT ATHENS, AND RECORDED THE FIRST DISCOVERER, AND FOUNDER OF THESE BATHES, EIGHT HVNDRED SIXTY AND THREE YEARES BEFORE CHRIST, THAT IS TWO THOWSAND FIVE HVNDRED THIRTY FIVE YEARS SINCE ANNO DOMINI 1672*

ANNÆ REGINÆ SACRVM 1618

ABOVE *Thomas Johnson's pen and ink drawing of 1675 shows the lively scene in the King's Bath. Described at the time as 'a seething pot', it was to be some years before decorum and elegance were introduced to the baths.*

'tastes like the water that boyles Eggs, has such a smell, but the nearer the pumpe you drinke it, the hotter and less offensive and more spiriteous'.

That tireless traveller and observer of life gave, in *Through England on a Side-Saddle,* a characteristically informative account of the baths and the procedures for bathing and drinking the waters. The pump at which she drank was in the gallery of the King's Bath, to the south-west of the Abbey. Communicating with the King's Bath, and separated by a wall and arch, was the more temperate Queen's Bath, named after another royal visitor,

Anne of Denmark, who had come in search of a cure for dropsy. At a little distance was the Leper's Bath, for 'lame and diseased poor people', which drew its water from the Hot Bath. Another was the Cross Bath, which adjoined the Queen's Bath and which, according to Celia Fiennes, was used mainly in the heat of summer:

> The Cross in the middle has seates round it for the
> Gentlemen to sitt and round the walls are arches with
> seates for the Ladyes – all stone, and the seate is stone and
> if you think the seat is too low they raise it with a coushon
> as they call it, another Stone, but indeed the water bears
> you up that the seate seemes as easy as a down coushon;
> before the Arch the Ladyes use to have a laced toilet hung
> up on the top of the Arch, and so to shelter their heads
> even to the water if they please: you generally set [*sic*] up
> to the neck in water.

BELOW Thomas Robins's watercolour of the King's Bath in the middle of the eighteenth century. The Pump Room's distinctive arched windows in the style of an orangery are visible on the left, and in the foreground are the chairs in which visitors were carried to and from the baths.

When Celia Fiennes revisited Bath some years later she noticed that the cross had become a memorial to the Catholic queen Mary of Modena. Upon this it became the custom to hang the crutches of invalids who had been cured by bathing in the Cross Bath:

Just in the midst a marble cross there stands
Which popish minds with pious awe commands,
Devoid itself of power to cure our woes,
Yet deck'd with monumental crutches, shows
What mighty cures that wondrous pool has done.

The baths were all open to the sky and, it was said, 'to the gaze of every footman'. Around the three main baths were galleries from which spectators could watch and converse with the bathers, with a place for the musicians.

BATHING IN THE WATERS

When she walked about the baths Celia Fiennes was sometimes accompanied by two guides, with two men going before her to clear a way. The spring water bubbled up fast and strong, and felt hot against the soles of her feet, especially in a part of the King's Bath that she called the 'Kitching', where there were seats. She saw people being pumped with water for lameness, and on their heads for paralysis: 'they put on a broad brimm'd hat with the crown cut out, so as the brims cast off the water from the face.'

The procedure for going to the baths, as described by the visiting antiquary Samuel Gale in 1705, was:

> for the gentlemen and ladies to dress themselves in
> their proper habits in their own apartments; the first
> in fine canvas waistcoats of a sandy colour, edged and
> trimmed with black ribbands or ferreting, and tied down
> before with strings of the same colour, having on canvas
> drawers and slippers, and a lawn linen cap; the latter in
> canvas gowns and petticoats, with pieces of lead affixed at
> the bottom, to keep them down under the water. Being
> thus dressed they are brought in chairs, sometimes close
> covered up in their morning gowns.

Gale's account continues:

> The ladies bring with them japanned bowls or basons, tied
> to their arms with ribbands, which swim upon the surface
> of the water, and are to keep their handkerchiefs, nosegays,
> perfumes, and spirits, in case the exhalations of the water
> should be too prevalent. The usual compliment, when any
> one goes into the bath, is to wish them a good bath; and

ABOVE *An original bathing chair of the eighteenth century in the collection of the Mineral Water Hospital (now the Royal National Hospital for Rheumatic Diseases). Staircases in the lodging houses of the period may have been designed with specially generous proportions to permit visitors to be carried in chairs all the way up to their rooms.*

the company, while bathing, generally regale themselves with chocolate.

Later, it became the practice to take a snuff-box into the baths; also patches, made of black silk and worn in imitation of beauty spots, 'tho' the Bath occasioning a little Perspiration, the Patches do not stick so kindly as they should'.

Taking up Celia Fiennes' description once again:

BELOW *The old Cross Bath, an engraving by John Fayram. In the Cross Bath 'is performed all the wanton dalliance imaginable,' wrote Ned Ward in 1700; 'languishing eyes, darting killing glances, tempting amorous postures attended by soft music, enough to provoke a vestal to forbidden pleasure, captivate a saint and charm a Jove.'*

When you go out of the bath you go within a door that leads to steps which you ascend by degrees, that are in the water, then the doore is shut which shuts down into the water a good way, so you are in a private place, where you still ascend severall more steps, and let your canvas drop off by degrees into the water, which your women guides takes off, and the meanetyme your maides flings [*sic*] a garment of flannell made like a nightgown with great sleeves over your head, and the guides take the taile and so pulls it on you just as you rise the steps, and your other garment drops off so you are wrapped up in the flannell and your nightgown is on top, your slippers, and so you are set in a Chaire which is brought into the roome which are called slips.

The slips had chimneys, and fires might be lit in them; even so they were described by Wood as 'rather cells for the dead than dressing-rooms for the living'.

The sedan chairs carrying the ladies to and from their lodgings were 'hermetically closed', in the words of a visitor from France, 'when the occupants were old, ugly or prudish, and artistically penetrable when they were finely formed'. Celia Fiennes complained that no control was exercised over the chairmen and that they imposed whatever fares they chose. If these were disputed, they would not let their customers out of the chair, 'though if it was raining they would open the top and let him or

her – often an invalid – be exposed to the wet, until in despair the charge was met'.

The Cross Bath was the most frequented by the fashionable of both sexes. Here, wrote Gale, 'with the greatest order and decency':

> the gentlemen keep to one side of the bath, and the ladies to the other. No gentleman whatever must presume to bathe in the ladies' district, under a pecuniary mulct, inflicted by the serjeants of the bath: the ladies are supposed to be so modest as not to come near the gentlemen.

A rather different picture was given by Daniel Defoe in his *Tour thro' the Whole Island of Great Britain*, published in 1724:

ABOVE *Bathers in the King's Bath wearing the wide-brimmed canvas hats commonly used there. The water bounced off the brim and kept the bathers' faces dry when they were being doused with water. The pen and wash drawing is by Grimm.*

the Ladies and Gentlemen pretend to keep some distance, and each to their proper side, but frequently mingle here too, as in the King and Queen's Bath, tho' not so often; and the place being but narrow, they converse freely, and talk, rally, make Vows, and sometimes Love.

Later in the century a scene of roistering bathers was described by Christopher Anstey in his light-hearted satire, *The New Bath Guide; or, Memoirs of the B—R—D Family in a series of Poetical Epistles*:

How the Ladies did giggle and set up their Clacks,
All the while an old Woman was rubbing their Backs!
Oh 'twas pretty to see them all put on their Flannels,
And then take the Water, like so many Spaniels.
And tho' all the while it grew hotter and hotter,
They swam, just as if they were hunting an Otter;
'Twas a glorious sight to behold the Fair Sex
All wading with Gentlemen up to their Necks,

ABOVE *Thomas Rowlandson's series of twelve satirical prints,* The Comforts of Bath, *was first published in 1798. The prints generally feature a gout-ridden old man and his pretty young wife experiencing the daily routine of life in Bath. This, the first plate, depicts a patient attended by three doctors.*

And view them so prettily tumble and sprawl
In a great smoking Kettle as big as our Hall:
And To-Day many Persons of Rank and Condition
Were boil'd by Command of an able Physician.

MEDICS AND QUACKS

By the beginning of the eighteenth century physicians, surgeons, apothecaries, midwives, dentists and purveyors of various forms of quackery were said to outnumber the patients. In a sly thrust at the doctors whose main place of practice was elsewhere, and who were in Bath only for the season, *The Tatler* reported that they had been directed to return home, and the stage coaches ordered to take them in before any other passengers until such time as there remained only two doctors to each patient.

Richard Steele, founder of *The Tatler*, giving a satirical account of the medical attentions he received, wrote that he had been cured of 'more distemper than I ever had in my life' by the good nature of physicians: 'They had almost killed me with their humanity.' Among the imaginary – and imaginative – restoratives and remedies he listed were:

BELOW *James Gillray's cartoon of a quack doctor of the late eighteenth century treating a patient with Perkins's Tractors. The invention of an American doctor, Elisha Perkins, the 'tractors' consisted of metal rods that were stroked over the skin as a cure for such disorders as gout, epilepsy and inflammations.*

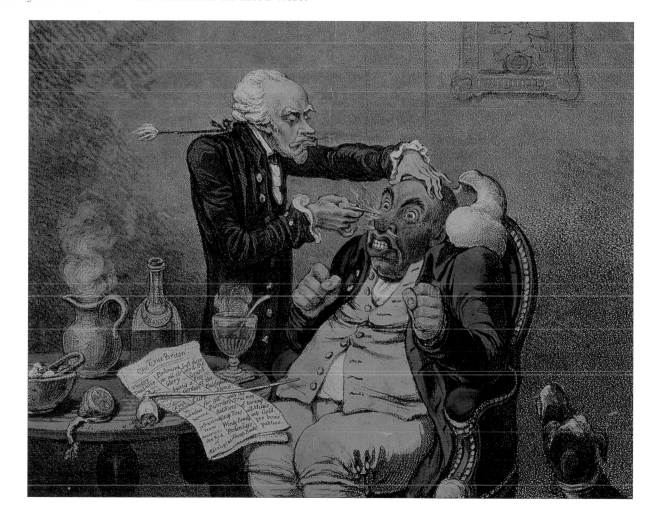

Live Hog Lice, Burnt Coke quenched in Aqua Vitæ, Red Coral, New Gathered Earth Worms, Live Toads, Black Tips of Crabs' Claws, Man's Skull, Elks' Hoofs, Leaves of Gold, Man's bones calcined, Inward Skin of a Capon's Gizzard, Goose Dung gather'd in the Spring Time, Dry'd in the Sun, the Stone of a Carp's Head, Unicorn's Horn, Boar's tooth, Jaw of a Pike, Sea Horse Tooth rasp'd, Frog's livers, white dung of a Peacock Dry'd, and Toads' and Vipers' flesh.

A humorous image of an apothecary going by the name of Stercorio appears in the anonymous poem *The Diseases of Bath*, published in 1737:

His raging Caustics flame upon his Nose,
With drowsy Poppies loaded are his Brows:
His cheeks puffed up with Arsinic, Gaul, and Sloth;

In the same poem the surgeon Jeremiah Peirce is commended for his humanity, rare honesty and sympathy, dealing 'but against his grain in blood and steel'. No mention is made, however, of the much-respected doctor William Oliver, inventor of the famous Bath Oliver biscuit (so plain as to be suitable for invalids) and author of *A Practical Essay on the Use and Abuse of Warm Bathing in Gouty Cases* of 1757. Both Peirce and Oliver were involved in the new Mineral Water Hospital, Peirce from the very beginning and Oliver when the hospital first opened its doors to patients.

The idea for the hospital dated from 1716, in which year Sir Joseph Jekyll, Master of the Rolls, Member of Parliament (champion of the Gin Act, which imposed a duty on the liquor and was thus un-popular with the poor) and philanthropist, started to raise money for the project. A committee of thirteen was set up to administer the charity, and it met once a month. Dr Peirce was one of the original members, as was the popular doctor George Cheyne, author of *An Essay on Health and Long Life*, which advocated restraint in the habits of eating and drinking, though at one time he himself weighed more than thirty-two stone.

At first the intention was to 'provide for poor lepers, cripples and other indigent persons resorting to Bath for cure, well recommended and not otherwise provided for'. The regulations confined treatment to the sick and needy who crowded in to the city and bothered the visitors. The inhabitants of Bath were not eligible, water from the health-giving springs being already available to them. Only in 1835 were the qualifications amended to admit any person who had not the means to receive treatment without charitable assistance.

Among those lending their support to the hospital plan were the Master of Ceremonies Richard Nash, the entrepreneur Ralph Allen and the London druggist Humphrey Thayer. Thayer, who owned land in Bath, had employed the services of the young architect John Wood, and it was to Wood that the committee turned to draw up plans for the hospital. It is notable that three of the men involved with the Mineral Water Hospital, Nash, Allen

ABOVE The Bath Esculapius, *a caricature of a Bath doctor etched by Matthew Darly in 1777. The glass that he holds is of the pattern used in the Pump Room for drinking the waters. Darly, who was a London engraver with a shop in the Strand, published a set of twenty-four 'Bath Worthies', small prints mounted on pasteboard.*

and Wood, played key roles in improving the physical and moral character of Bath during the eighteenth century, and in creating England's most fashionable resort.

Many years were spent in acquiring a site for the hospital building, and it was not until 1737, when the playhouse closed, that a suitable piece of land, in the northern part of the city, became available. In 1742 Mr Peirce was appointed senior surgeon at the Mineral Water Hospital and Dr Oliver honorary physician, and the first patients were admitted. Apart from relieving the suffering of the chronically sick whose parishes could barely afford to support them, and who were therefore kept 'in a continual state of infirmity, by a small allowance at home', another reason for establishing the hospital was so that the doctors could test the efficacy of the waters on their patients and improve treatments. One hundred and ten cases were admitted at a time, each one having a certificate from the parish, signed by two justices, attesting to the poverty of his or her circumstances. They presented themselves also with:

three pounds caution-money, if from any part of England or Wales; but if the patient comes from Scotland or Ireland, then the caution-money, to be deposited before admission, is the sum of five pounds.

Soldiers could come with a certificate from their commanding officers and proof that they would be taken back into their regiments when discharged from the hospital, whatever their condition. They brought with them three pounds caution-money. Goldsmith explained that the money was to defray the expense of returning the patients after they had been discharged or of burying them, should the treatment prove unsuccessful.

BATHING AND PUMPING IN GEORGIAN TIMES

John Penrose, a clergyman visiting Bath in 1766 with his wife and eldest daughter Fanny, was attended for his gout by an apothecary named Haviland, who had been recommended by his own doctor in Cornwall, Dr Coode. Penrose was advised to drink a quarter of a pint of the waters at seven and again at twelve. At first he was prescribed a mixture of the Cross Bath waters and the King's Bath

LEFT Brass identity medallions worn by patients in the eighteenth century, as shown by the man and child in the painting on page 36. Patients were sent from all over the British Isles, and broadsheets advertising the hospital's services and admission rules were distributed to parishes throughout the country.

waters, and later water taken solely from the King's Bath. Mr Haviland passed on to him the received wisdom that the water was more effective as a cure when it was drunk as hot as possible from the pump and as close as possible to its source. After the reverend gentleman had been receiving treatment for a while it occurred to him that the apothecary might not approve of his eating hot bread for breakfast. He was greatly relieved, on a chance encounter with him, by the exchange: 'How much do you eat? – Very Well. – Then eat it. – But many advise me against it. – Pugh!' Mr Haviland was 'one of Ten Thousand', was the clergyman's satisfied conclusion. Penrose intended to stay for six weeks, but Haviland claimed that his patient had received 'so much Benefit as he never saw a like Instance' and that he should remain in Bath for a fortnight longer.

On a second visit, the following year, Penrose was advised by Mr Haviland to chew rhubarb twice a week, 'enough to give me two or three Motions. I think I am bettering; my Stools are most substantial, and not white as they were.' A few days later he wished it to be reported to Dr Coode that his 'Yellowness or

BELOW *The King's Bath in Plate VII of Rowlandson's* The Comforts of Bath. *'Judge SCRUB, and the worthy Old Councellor PEST/ Join'd Issue at once and went in with the rest'. Christopher Anstey's verses are similar in satirical content to Rowlandson's illustrations.*

Paleness is rather abated', but that otherwise the symptoms of his disorder had not changed.

Lord Chesterfield, seeking a cure for deafness, also found that his condition had not improved. 'I have tried these waters in every possible way,' he wrote; 'I have bathed my head; pumped it; introduced the stream, and sometimes drops of water, into my ears'; but all was in vain.

Matthew Bramble, in Tobias Smollett's novel *The Expedition of Humphry Clinker*, doubted most strongly that bathing was conducive to health. He felt his blood run cold, he wrote to Dr

BELOW *Detail of people waiting in line for glasses of the water, from* Taking the Waters at the Pump Room, Bath, *1784, a watercolour by Humphrey Repton.*

Lewis, at the thought of the perspiration and 'scrophulous ulcers' that might be running in the waters of the King's Bath. 'To purify myself from all such contamination, I went to the duke of Kingston's Bath, and there I was almost suffocated for want of free air; the place was so small, and the steam so stifling.' The Roman baths were discovered during the building of the Duke of Kingston's bath in 1755. The Duke's comprised five small covered baths, so small that it was only just possible to turn round in them, and were supplied by the same springs as the King's and Queen's Baths; adjoining them were steam rooms. People went to these more expensive and exclusive baths for the sake of privacy and so that they could bathe naked.

'I am now as much afraid of drinking as of bathing,' continued the gouty and irascible Bramble:

> for, after a long conversation with the doctor about the construction of the pump and the cistern, it is very far from being clear to me, that the patients in the Pump Room don't swallow the scourings of the bathers. I can't help suspecting that there is, or may be, some regurgitation from the bath into the cistern of the pump. In that case, what a delicate beverage is every day quaffed by the drinkers; medicated with the sweat, and dirt, and dandriff, and the abominable discharges of various kinds, from twenty different diseased bodies, parboiling in the kettle below.

He was even more alarmed by a visit to the spring supplying the new Private Baths:

> I at once perceived something extraordinary in the taste and smell, and, upon inquiry, I find that the Roman baths in this quarter were found covered by an old burying ground belonging to the Abbey, through which, in all probability, the water drains its passage: so that as we drink the decoction of living bodies at the Pump-room, we swallow the strainings of rotten bones and carcases at the private bath.

Smollett was himself a doctor and felt some bitterness towards Bath, having failed as a young man to establish a practice for himself there. His criticism of the condition of the baths and claims that the waters provided no greater benefit than any other natural water set him against the establishment. He also became involved in a notorious scandal surrounding Archibald Cleland,

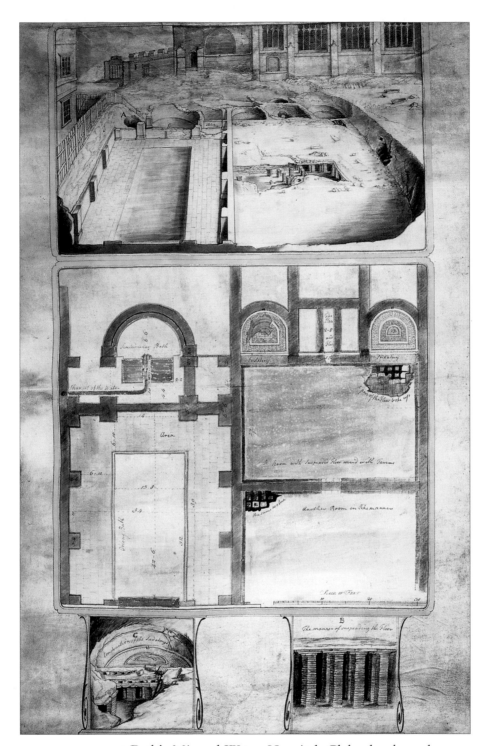

a surgeon at Bath's Mineral Water Hospital. Cleland, whom he defended against the hospital authorities, was accused of under-taking unauthorized medical examinations of the patients in the care of other doctors, examinations of an indecent nature.

Despite complaints about the unsatisfactory condition of the baths and the impurity of the water at the pumps, there were

ABOVE *William Hoare's drawing of the Roman baths, unearthed during the building of the Duke of Kingston's bath in 1755.*

many who were convinced of the efficacy of the water treatments. Samuel Cowper, Dean of Durham, wrote to his brother:

> Those yellow-faces you complain of at the Pump-Room,
> tho' they are disagreeable to look at, are worth watching,
> for you will find most of them in a few weeks brighten up
> to a healthy red, so as hardly to be known again; and look
> as happy as they did dejected and miserable before.

The local poet Mary Chandler, in praise of 'Jordan's stream' (a reference to Dr Jorden) and the beneficial effects obtained from the waters by visitors to Bath, wrote:

> Thy waters have recalled the fleeting Breath,
> Repriev'd the Wretch by him resign'd to Death:
> Giv'n Vigour to the Spirits, Ease from Pain,
> Made the Lame walk, and clear'd the clouded Brain:
> Was'd in the Waves Distempers die away,
> And ruddy Health returns like rising Day.

BEAU NASH
KING OF BATH

IN 1702, THE YEAR OF her accession to the throne, Queen Anne paid a visit to Bath with her consort Prince George. When last she came she had been shown no special respect on the insistence of her sister Mary, but now she was received with great display and ceremony, her escort including a hundred young men of the city, uniformed and armed, and two hundred young women dressed as Amazons. The city and surrounding villages overflowed with visitors, as they did when she came the following year. Through royal patronage Bath became a fashionable resort, frequented not only by the sick but by people of wealth and distinction in pursuit of pleasure and diversion.

THE EARLY LIFE OF RICHARD NASH

Attracted by the new-found popularity of the place, Richard Nash came to Bath in 1705 with a party of young men. 'It is a matter of very little importance who were the parents, or what was the education of a man who owed so little of his advancement to either,' wrote Oliver Goldsmith in his memoir of Nash, though he was in fact the son of a Swansea bottlemaker and had paid brief attendance at Jesus College, Oxford. He distinguished himself at Oxford by 'an extraordinary and precocious genius for intrigue and gallantry', and before he was seventeen he had got himself into at least a dozen 'delicate dilemmas'. Later, as a student of law at the Middle Temple, 'he spread the little gold he had, in the most ostentatious manner.' He was one of those, it was said, 'who spend more in chair hire, than housekeeping; and prefer a bow from a Lord, to a dinner from a Commoner.'

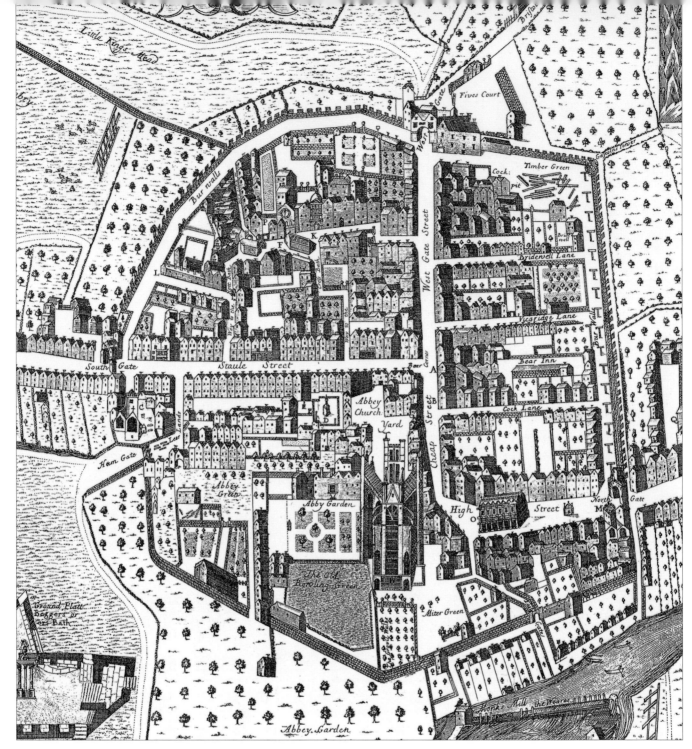

He was at the time of his appearance in Bath thirty years old, without money and without the useful talents for acquiring any. By profession a gamester, he went from day to day, feeling the vicissitudes of rapture and anguish, in proportion to the fluctuations of fortune'. He was 'if not a brilliant, at least an easy companion and he had what was described as 'the spirit of frolick'. The story is told that once, having lost all his money in York, he agreed for fifty guineas to stand at the great door of the Minster in a blanket as the people were coming out of church. The Dean, passing by, recognized him:

What, cried the Divine, Mr Nash in masquerade? *Only a Yorkshire penance Mr Dean, for keeping bad company*, says Nash, pointing to his companions.

Some time after this he had won a wager 'of still greater consequence', by riding naked through a village on a cow. He had come to Bath eager to try his luck at the gaming-tables.

NASH'S ARRIVAL IN BATH

Since Queen Anne's visit, Captain Webster had been appointed Master of Ceremonies by the Corporation of Bath, and although he had established a series of subscription balls at the town hall and improved the arrangements for gambling, which was by now one of the principal attractions of Bath, the amusements provided were neither elegant nor conducted with delicacy. There was 'no machinery for introductions'; men smoked in the presence of the ladies who met for tea or chocolate and cards in a canvas booth; gentlemen appeared at the dances in top-boots, and ladies in white aprons; and the sedan chairmen were rude and disrespectful. John Wood wrote that 'The city was in itself mean and contemptible.'

In the seven weeks of the season Nash was said to have won a thousand pounds at the tables. He 'soon made himself conspicuous by the splendour of his equipage, his trim attire, courteous manners, and invincible good humour'. Gaining the regard of Webster, Nash was appointed his aide. One night a quarrel

BELOW *Detail from* West Prospect of Bath Bridge, *an early eighteenth-century view of the city by Bernard Lens. A visitor to Bath, Lens was on hand to draw studies of the Minerva head when it was discovered.*

ABOVE *A view of the Old Rooms and North Parade in 1780 drawn by Benjamin Morris. The building in the centre with the three circular attic windows was the ballroom for Lindsey's Assembly Rooms. In the adjacent terrace were lodgings, gaming rooms and, so scandal suggested, a brothel.*

between Webster and another player ended in a duel in which Webster was killed. Nash was appointed his successor as 'King of Bath' and at once set about correcting what he saw as the provincial character of the place.

EARLY REFORMS

One of Nash's first measures, acting on behalf of the Corporation, was to raise the quality of the entertainments by engaging a band of musicians to play in the public places, raising a subscription of one guinea to defray the expense and a further two guineas for the lighting and sweeping of the rooms. He next ordered the lodging-houses to be refitted and imposed a regular tariff. He also tried to curb the exorbitant demands of the chairmen.

It was perhaps at Nash's instigation that a subscription was raised for the rebuilding of the road that led from Lansdown Hill into the city. That the Corporation applied to Parliament 'for a superior power' to oblige householders to keep clear from rubbish, ashes and rubble all the streets, alleys and public ways outside their properties, and between 14 September and 25 March to light those same areas at night with candles, lights or lanterns, may have been due to Nash's initiative as well. Failure to comply resulted in a fine, part of the money being paid over for the relief of the poor. Night watchmen were introduced in a further

ABOVE *An eighteenth-century detail by the door of a house. The snuffer was used by link-boys to extinguish their torches.*

attempt to reassure visitors, and vagrants and beggars were cleared from the streets. Where previously there had been only one season in Bath, to improve the city's finances Nash decreed that there should be two: from March to June and October to Christmas.

A room to provide shelter for those drinking the waters had been begun in Webster's time, and a grand opening was arranged by Nash at its completion in 1706, for which the song in honour of Bladud was composed. Nash rented the Pump Room from the Corporation and put it in the hands of a Pumper, who paid Nash for the position and made his living from tips.

In 1708 a room for playing at dice and gambling was built, with Nash's encouragement, by Thomas Harrison. At Harrison's Rooms, which would later be enlarged to include a ballroom, and were afterwards known by the name of subsequent owners – Mrs Hayes (afterwards Lady Hawley), Gyde, Simpson – a ball was held on Tuesdays during the season. From 1729, when the building was put up, a ball was held on Fridays at the rooms built by Humphrey Thayer. Thayer's was later known as Lindsey's (after the singer turned casino mistress and madam, to whom the building was let) and later still as Wiltshire's (after it came into the hands of the family of hauliers). The scene was set for public assemblies.

RULES AND REGULATIONS

It was in the Pump Room that Nash posted up for all to see his famous code of behaviour. There were eleven rules in all, which were 'in general religiously observed by his subjects', according to

BELOW *A pen and wash drawing by Grimm of chairmen celebrating in the Orange Grove. Under Nash, the annual licensing of chairmen was very carefully controlled.*

RIGHT *Beau Nash painted by William Hoare in 1749 wearing his white beaver hat over a full black wig. Hoare presented this painting to the Corporation in 1762, the year after Nash's death. Like other kings, Nash had 'his mistresses, flatterers, enemies and calumniators,' wrote Goldsmith.*

Goldsmith, and 'executed by him with impartiality, neither rank nor fortune shielded the refractory from his resentment'. They were written in a manner that Goldsmith construed as intended 'for wit'.

'That a Visit of Ceremony at coming to Bath and another at going away,' read the first rule, 'is all that is expected or desired, by Ladies of Quality and Fashion;—except Impertinents'. On arrival in the city, weary from a journey by coach that from London, even at the beginning of the eighteenth century, would have taken more than thirty-six hours, visitors were greeted by a peal of the Abbey bells, then at their lodgings by the city's strolling musicians. The disturbance to the peace might have offended the sick, but 'Invalids are fond of news, and upon the first sound of the bells, every body sends out to enquire for whom they ring.' Later, they received a visit from the Master of Ceremonies in person.

Gossip was rife, in the Assembly Rooms, in the Pump Room, coffee houses and on the parades. The last rules read:

> That all Whisperers of Lies and Scandal be taken for their Authors. That all Repeaters of such Lies and Scandal be shun'd by all Company;—except such as have been guilty of the same Crime. N.B. Several Men of no Character, Old Women and Young Ones of Questioned Reputation, are great Authors of Lies in this place, being of the Sect of Levellers.

Five of the rules concerned the conduct of ladies and gentlemen at a ball. Goldsmith described the proceedings as formalized by Nash:

> He opened each ball, by taking out two persons of the highest distinction present to dance a minuet; when the minuet was ended, the lady returned to her seat, and Nash brought the gentleman a new partner; this ceremony was observed with every succeeding couple, every gentleman being obliged to dance with two ladies.

After about two hours the country dances began, ladies of quality, according to their rank, standing up first. A short interval was then allowed for rest, 'and for the gentlemen to help their partners to tea':

> When this was over, the dancing continued till eleven, and, as soon as the clock had struck, Nash came into the room, and ordered the music to stop, by holding up his finger: the dances were of course discontinued, and some time being allowed for the company to grow cool, the ladies were handed to their chairs.

When Princess Amelia, daughter of George II, applied to him for one more dance after the music had come to an end, even she was forced to submit to Nash's authority.

He would tolerate no snobbishness, the 'tincture of Gothic haughtiness' referred to by Goldsmith, which kept the nobility apart from the gentry. If he observed a lady of quality touching the back of the hand of a social inferior while dancing, instead of clasping it, he would at once reprove the offender.

He forbade altogether the carrying of swords, which 'tore the ladies cloaths, and frightened them, by sometimes appearing on trifling occasions'.

ABOVE *A miniature of Princess Amelia by Samuel Cotes. It was said that she had set her heart on marrying Frederick the Great, but she remained unmarried and was a frequent visitor to Bath during the season.*

His chief care was employed,
In preventing obscenity or impudence
From offending the modesty or the morals
Of the Fair Sex.
And in banishing from their assemblies
Tumult, clamour, and abuse.

ARBITER ELEGANTARIUM

'Beau' Nash, as he was called, in the early years of his reign as King of Bath, set a fine example of elegance in dress. On his head he wore a full-bottom black wig and a large cream-coloured tricorne hat, tipped well forward and lightly grazing his right eyebrow. His brown coat was frogged and edged with lace. Beneath he wore a waistcoat embroidered with flowers, unbuttoned to reveal a quantity of fine lace. As he grew older he mixed the fashion of the day with the fashion of his youth, continuing to wear a diamond buckle in his stock and a diamond star to pin back the flap of his hat

He was large and awkward, with harsh, strong and unsymmetrical features, yet as a young man:

> There was a whimsical refinement in his person, dress, and behaviour, which was habitual to and sat so easily upon him that no stranger who came to Bath ever expresses any surprise at his uncommon manner and appearance.

His swashbuckling manner and swaggering gait made him conspicuous wherever he went within his 'kingdom'. When he made the journey each year to Tunbridge Wells his equipage was sumptuous. He travelled 'in a post chariot and six greys, with out-riders, footmen, French horns, and every other appendage of expensive parade'.

No inelegance in the attire of others went unrebuked – he was indeed the *arbiter elegantarium* – and when the Duchess of Queensberry appeared at a ball in an apron, Nash stripped it from her and threw it to the back of the room with the comment, 'None but *Abigails* appear in white aprons.' To make his views clear to the 'Trollops and Slatterns' who appeared unsuitably dressed, he first composed a satirical poem ridiculing their rustic attire and then organized a puppet show in which Punch appears dressed as a country squire in

BELOW *A gentleman of fashion in the mid-eighteenth century. The wearing of swords was banned in Bath, partly, John Wood related in his* Description of Bath, *because of the frequent skirmishes between the chairmen and their passengers.*

boots and spurs to court his mistress and is kicked off the stage in disgust by her. From this time very few ventured to appear like Punch since, according to *The Gentleman's Magazine*, 'the moment a pair of boots entered the place, the whole ridiculous scene recurred to every one that had seen it, and all the company were in a laugh.'

BENEVOLENCE AND GALLANTRY
OF THE BEAU

At the gaming-tables, 'A thousand instances might be given of his integrity', and 'he defrauded no man, nor would he, knowingly, suffer any man to be defrauded by others'. Whenever he found a novice in the hands of a sharper, Nash never failed to warn him of his danger, and whenever he found a person willing to play, but ignorant of the game, he would offer his services and play for him.

A story is told by Goldsmith of 'a gentleman of broken fortune', who, standing behind Nash's chair as he was playing a game of Piquet for two hundred pounds:

ABOVE AND BELOW *'The Exact Dress of the Head from the Life at Court, Opera, Theatre, Park etc.', 1727, by Bernard Lens. Nash was famous for insisting upon correct manners and dress, in imitation of those at court.*

and observing with what indifference he won the money, could not avoid whispering these words to another who stood by; 'heavens! how happy would all that money make me!' *Nash*, overhearing him, clapp'd the money into his hand; and cried, *go and be happy.*

He played a part in exposing many a scheming libertine, and more than one heiress owed to him her escape from the snares of penniless adventurers. From the frivolous and feckless young man about Oxford and London, the Beau had become the honest protector of innocence and the guardian of reputations:

> Long reigned the great Nash, this omnipotent lord,
> Respected by youth, and by parents adored;
> For him not enough at a ball to reside,
> The unwary and beautiful nymph would he guide;
> Oft tell her a tale, how the credulous maid
> By man, by perfidious man, is betrayed.

He was continually raising subscriptions among the visitors for one cause or another: for colliers and weavers during a particularly severe winter, and for a clergyman living with a wife and six children on thirty pounds a year, whom he had unkindly called 'Dr Cullender' on account of the many holes in his coat and stockings. His principal benefactions were directed towards the setting up of the Mineral Water Hospital, to which he contributed no less than a fifth of the sum raised. Every opportunity was taken to generate funds, and Nash, apart from arranging subscription concerts and balls, was not ashamed to make a collection standing in the Abbey with a basin; nor to extract money from individuals amidst the frivolities in the Assembly Rooms. Famously, he teased the Duchess of Marlborough into parting with a handful of guineas, after she had protested that she had none in her pocket. 'Charity hides a multitude of sins,' the Beau said as he counted out coins from his own purse on her behalf. 'Twenty-one, twenty-two, twenty-three . . . Madam, you will never die with doing good; and if you do it will be the better for you.'

RIGHT *Frederick, Prince of Wales, after the portrait by Jean-Baptiste Van Loo, painted at Cliveden. The prince would have endeared himself to Nash by his generosity to the Mineral Water Hospital. He donated £100 on its opening and made a further contribution in 1745.*

Published by G. Speren June 1757 according to Act of Parliament

Another contributor to the hospital was Frederick, Prince of Wales, who visited Bath in 1738 on his way to Cliveden, four years after the city had been honoured with a visit from the Prince of Orange. Frederick presented Nash with a magnificent gold snuff-box, and thereafter it became the fashion to donate snuff-boxes to him. In gratitude for the two princes' patronage of the watering place, Nash erected obelisks in their honour.

The Corporation thereupon determined to erect a portrait of Nash, between the busts of Isaac Newton and Alexander Pope in Wiltshire's Rooms. This gave rise to the caustic epigram:

> The picture, placed the busts between,
> Adds to the satire strength;
> Wisdom and Wit are little seen,
> But Folly's at full length.

The Beau, though the object of ridicule, was at the height of his fame, honoured and admired for his generosity, gallantry and wit. One of his maxims was that good humour and fine clothes were enough to ruin a nunnery; but that 'flummery', or the art of saying nothings, was worth both together. Women, he said, dote upon lively nonsense, so talk to them in the language they best understand. The instant you begin to converse rationally with them all is lost, and this is the reason learned men make indifferent lovers.

ABOVE AND BELOW LEFT *An engraved design for a fan by George Speren showing the obelisk erected in what became known as the Orange Grove to mark the successful outcome of the treatment undertaken by William, Prince of Orange, in 1734. The obelisk in Queen Square was erected in 1738 to commemorate the visit of Frederick, Prince of Wales. It was commissioned by Nash from John Wood.*

LEFT *Detail from a watercolour of the Pump Room in the 1790s by John Nixon. It shows the marble statue of Beau Nash, thought to be by Joseph Plura, and the Tompion clock, both of which were in the original Pump Room during Nash's lifetime.*

NASH'S LAST YEARS

The decline in Nash's reputation and in his fortunes began simultaneously, at about the time severe penalties were enacted against gambling. In 1739 such games as Faro, Basset, Hazard and Ace of Spades were prohibited, and in 1740 the law was strengthened to include any game 'with numbers thereon'. EO (Evens and Odds, a form of Roulette) was invented to evade the law, and Nash was party to setting up tables for the play of the new game, first in Tunbridge Wells, of which town he had been appointed Master of Ceremonies in 1735, and then in Bath. It was when, through financial necessity, he sought redress in a lawsuit for the money owed to him through his involvement in introducing EO to the gaming-rooms that Nash's pecuniary interests in the gambling that took place at Bath were revealed. He appeared now not as the conductor but as one who shared part of the spoil at the tables, and for this he lost the people's esteem.

Even in old age, though peevish and fretful, and judged a bore for his repetition of stories of a daring and glamorous youth, the

Beau's wit never entirely deserted him. Sent some medicine by the stout Dr Cheyne, he was up and well when the doctor called the next day. To the claim that Nash was better as a result of following the doctor's prescription, the patient replied, 'Egad, if I had, I should have broken my neck, for I flung it out of the upstairs window', or so it was related in *The Valetudinarian's Bath Guide*. Cheyne was a strong advocate of vegetarianism: his design, Nash said, 'was to send half the world grazing, like Nebuchadnezzar'. At one of their meetings, the doctor complained that Nash 'behaved like other brutes, and laid down as soon as he had filled his belly'. 'Very true,' retorted Nash, 'and this prescription I had from a neighbour's cow, who is a better physician than you, and a superior judge of plants, notwithstanding you have written so learnedly on the vegetable diet.'

Towards the end, Nash was forced to leave his large house in St John's Court for a smaller one in Saw Close. He sold his collection of snuff-boxes. As his health declined, Juliana Papjoy, known as the 'Bishopstrowe belle' and the last of his mistresses, whom Nash had dismissed through lack of funds, came back to care for him. The Corporation, mindful of the benefits that the Beau had brought to the city, voted him ten pounds a month for the rest of his life.

Nash died on 3 February 1761 at the age of eighty-seven. The Corporation granted fifty pounds for the burying of their sovereign with proper respect, and in November of the following year *The Gentleman's Magazine* gave an account of his lying in state and the procession from his house to the Abbey:

> the charity girls two and two preceded, next the boys of
> the charity school, singing a solemn occasional hymn. Next
> marched the city music, and his own band, sounding at
> proper intervals a dirge. Three clergymen immediately
> preceded the coffin, which was adorned with sable plumes,
> and the pall supported by the six senior aldermen. The
> masters of the assembly rooms followed as chief mourners;
> the beadles of that hospital, which he had contributed so
> largely to endow, went next; and last of all, the poor
> patients themselves, the lame, the emaciated, and the
> feeble, followed their old benefactor to his grave, shedding
> unfeigned tears, and lamenting themselves in him.

Dr Oliver, Nash's friend and business partner, and Dr King, who like others of his profession had profited much from Nash's prudent rule as King of Bath, wrote generous memorials of the man who 'erected the city of Bath into a province of pleasure'.

THE BUILDING OF GEORGIAN BATH

ABOVE *Detail of typically elegant plasterwork from the ceiling of a room on the first floor of No. 16 in the Crescent, The Royal Crescent hotel.*

LEFT *Royal Crescent, built by John Wood the Younger and completed in 1775. The long row of uniform buildings, ranged in elliptical form, has always astonished the visitor with its majesty and grave simplicity.*

WHEN RICHARD NASH arrived in Bath in 1705, he had found 'no elegant buildings, no open streets, nor uniform squares'. There were few places to stay and, some twenty years later, the lodgings still left much to be desired, as described by John Wood. In his two-volume *Essay towards a Description of Bath*, first published in 1742–3, he wrote:

> About the year 1727, the Boards of the Dining Rooms and most other Floors were made of a Brown Colour with Soot and small Beer to hide the Dirt, as well as their own Imperfections; and if the Walls of any of the Rooms were covered with Wainscot, it was with such as was mean and never Painted: The Chimney-Pieces, Hearths and Slabbs were all of Free Stone, and these were daily cleaned with a particular White-wash, which, by paying Tribute to every thing that touched it, soon rendered the brown Floors like the Stary Firmament.

The principal rooms were cheaply furnished with rush-seated chairs, and oak tables and chests of drawers.

As time passed the buildings were improved:

> thatch'd coverings were exchanged to such as were tiled, low and obscure lights were turned into elegant sash windows . . . the houses were raised to five or more stories in height, and every one was lavish in ornaments . . .

Inside, there were wainscoted and painted walls, marble chimney-pieces and brass chimney and door furniture, carpets on the floors, and tables and chests of drawers of walnut and mahogany. Household articles made from wool and linen were replaced 'with such as was more fit for Gentlemens Capital Seats, than Houses appropriated for common Lodgings', so that the lodging houses had become 'suitable even for People of the highest Rank'. At the end of his preface Wood wrote:

> To make a just Comparison between the Publick Accommodations of *Bath* at this time, and one and twenty Years back, the best Chambers for Gentlemen were then just what the Garrets for Servants now are.

The Corporation was slow, too, in playing their part in improving the public amenities – the baths themselves, in particular. It was Ralph Allen, an entrepreneur, and John Wood, the architect and writer, who, with Richard Nash, saw what Bath might and should

BELOW The Four Worthies, *a painting of four men who played prominent roles in the building of Bath. On the left is Richard Jones, Clerk of Works to Ralph Allen, who sits opposite Robert Gay, a London surgeon who inherited the Manor of Walcot and therefore much valuable building land. Standing beside Gay is the architect John Wood.*

become. Together they are judged responsible for creating the greatest of all Georgian cities.

THE EARLY CAREER OF RALPH ALLEN

Ralph Allen arrived in Bath at the age of eighteen in 1712. As Deputy Postmaster, he was in a position to see that the postal system as it was then organized was inefficient and frequently abused. Over several years, he reformed the 'cross-road' and 'bye-way' system for delivering letters, and was granted a contract, which was renewed periodically for the rest of his life, that benefited both the Post Office and himself.

Looking for ways to invest his money, Allen realized that there was now a great demand for stone suitable for building work. In 1727 he bought the stone quarries at Combe Down on the outskirts of Bath. Three years previously a subscription had been opened by John Hobbs, a deal merchant of Bristol, to extend the navigation of the River Avon from Bristol to Bath. Soon, stone could be shipped from Bath to Bristol, and thence by sea to other parts of the country.

Wood gave a very good account of Allen's steely determination to make his quarries, and thus Bath stone, an economic proposition and 'encourage consumption of it'. Allen did the first by reforming the employment arrangements of the stonecutters:

BELOW *Two architectural details that demonstrate the fine quality of carving that could be achieved in Bath stone: left, from Rosewell House, Kingsmead Square, attributed to John Strahan, 1736; right, cornice and Corinthian pilaster from Queen Square by John Wood, 1729–36.*

instead of paying them for piecework, he paid them wages for regular hours each week, thus reducing the time they spent going up and down the hill to their homes in Bath. In reducing the total wage bill, he was able to reduce the price of the worked stone. In a more radical measure, he employed John Wood to design housing for his workers on top of Combe Down so they could live close to the quarries. He also constructed proper sheds in the yard so that the men could work under cover in all weathers.

The stone was originally carted down the hill to the river in horse-drawn wagons, but Allen soon improved the procedure by introducing a method of transport he had heard was being used by 'gentlemen in the North of England'. Colliery owners sent coal down from the hills to the River Tyne in heavy trucks that ran along rails. Allen sent off for a model of the carriages and copied the system for his stone. The loaded trucks were set in motion along the rails by horses, and brakes fitted to the trucks controlled their speed to keep the horses ahead of them on the journey downhill. The footpath alongside the tramway became a favourite walk for Bathonians.

With the same determination, Allen set out to prove that his Bath stone was as fine as Portland stone. He was keen to acquire a slice of the lucrative London market. However, in this venture

BELOW   *Detail from Samuel and Nathaniel Buck's panorama of Bath, published in 1734, which shows Ralph Allen's stoneyard and wharf at Widcombe on the banks of the Avon.*

ABOVE *An engraving of 1752 by Anthony Walker of Prior Park, the seat of Ralph Allen Esq. The house was sited close to Allen's tramway for transporting stone from the quarry and was designed to exhibit the excellence of his stone.*

he met implacable opposition from several of the leading architects of the day, in particular from Colen Campbell and Nicholas Hawksmoor, his opponents in the capital 'maliciously comparing the stone to Cheshire Cheese, liable to breed maggots that would soon devour it'. This was in spite of a meeting held at Salters' Hall in London in the spring of 1728, to which Allen and John Wood took samples of the stone in an attempt to put down the opposition and win the contract for Greenwich Hospital. Wood felt that Campbell exposed his prejudices when he inadvertently picked out Bath stone as the best.

JOHN WOOD AND QUEEN SQUARE

John Wood was born in Bath in 1704 and followed his father into the building trade. He worked for Lord Bingley on the house and in the grounds of Bramham Park in Yorkshire, and in the mid 1720s was acting as surveyor in London for the Duke of Chandos's Cavendish Square. He had by this time absorbed the principles of English Palladianism, a version of the sixteenth-century Andrea Palladio's style of classical architecture.

While still engaged on these works, Wood's thoughts turned to Bath and 'towards the Improvement of the City by Building':

> for this Purpose I procured a Plan of the Town, which was sent me into Yorkshire, in the summer of the Year 1725, where I, at my leisure Hours, formed one Design for the Ground, at the North West Corner of the City.

This land belonged to Robert Gay, Lord of the Manor of Walcot and an eminent London surgeon, who had been MP for Bath. Wood had another plan, 'for the Land, on the North East side of the Town and River', on the Earl of Essex's estate. These were alternative designs, for each included:

> a grand Place of Assembly, to be called the Royal Forum of Bath; another Place, no less magnificent, for the Exhibition of Sports, to be called the Grand Circus; and a third Place, of equal State with either of the former, for the Practice of Medicinal Exercises, to be called the Imperial Gymnasium of the City, from a Work of that kind, taking its Rise at first in Bath, during the Time of the Roman Emperors.

In London, Wood contacted the two owners of the land in question. His plans lay under consideration for a year. Then, in November 1726, he became Robert Gay's agent, with authority

ABOVE *Thomas Malton's watercolour of Queen Square in 1784, with the north 'palace' façade on the right of the painting. The large town house set back in the centre of the west side of the square was first lived in by Dr William Oliver.*

to enter into agreements with anyone willing to build a new street of houses. The first of these new streets begun by Wood was known as Barton Street and eventually as Gay Street.

In the following January he contracted with the Duke of Chandos to build a 'court of houses' as lodgings on the site of St John's Hospital, of which the Duke had acquired the lease. The Duke did not find Wood's work on this speculative investment satisfactory. He had failed to install ten water-closets properly, and the Duke did not employ him again.

In May 1727 Wood settled in Bath. The Corporation viewed with scepticism Wood's grandiose ideas for the creation of a new town situated outside the medieval city walls. Undeterred, he put forward a plan for the old town, but this was considered 'chimerical' and was duly rejected. Wood then decided on the courageous step of building a great residential square, taking on much of the risk himself.

The first attempt to unify a row of terrace houses to simulate a 'palace' front had been Colen Campbell, in his design of 1725 for the east side of Grosvenor Square in London. The scheme was not carried out, however, as the speculative builder balked at the cost. Wood's design for the north side of Queen Square is the realization of Campbell's plan, and the first application of Palladian architecture to an urban square. It was to set the style for subsequent squares and terraces built during the Georgian period throughout Britain and North America. In the architect's own words:

> it stands upon rising ground, faces those who come from
> the city into the square; and soars above the other buildings
> with a sprightliness, which gives it the elegance and
> grandeur of the body of a stately palace.

The Queen Square palace front is composed of a fine central pediment crowning the house in the middle, which is five bays wide. The pair of end houses, with an attic storey above the entablature, act as terminal pavilions.

Wood intended that the east and west sides of the square should be uniform. The east side was carried out as planned, but various constraints meant that the west side finally took the form of a large central mansion set back from the building line, flanked by a pair of houses. Wood was more successful than his contemporaries in imposing uniform elevations, though. He achieved this by forcing the various builders who took individual leases to

work to an agreed drawing. It soon became normal practice for a copy of the design to become part of the legal documentation accompanying the lease.

The financial arrangement that lies behind the building of Queen Square is of interest, as it was the system used on other occasions during the building of eighteenth-century Bath. Wood took a series of ninety-nine-year leases from the ground landlord, Robert Gay. The first lease was granted in November 1728 and was for two plots on the south and east sides of the square. Each had a frontage of 100 feet (30 metres) and a depth of 150 feet (46 metres). The ground rent for each was £20 *per annum*, which had been calculated by fixing a rate of two shillings per foot and multiplying that by the width of the site's main frontage.

In two years starting from September 1729, Wood granted ninety-eight-year sub-leases to builders for the erection of houses on both the plots. Also during this time, Wood leased the rest of the land around the square from Robert Gay, and sub-let plots to different builders. By 1736 all twenty-seven houses in Queen Square had been built, using Bath stone from Ralph Allen's quarries. Gay and his heirs were now in possession of ground rents worth £137 *per annum*, and they would eventually, when the leases expired, own the houses. Wood and his heirs obtained an income of £305 1s. *per annum* from those who took sub-leases from him. Clearly, Wood made a handsome profit.

ABOVE *A mid-eighteenth-century view across the Avon and up to Prior Park on the hill in the distance, a painting by Thomas Ross. The river was an essential feature of the landscape as seen from the house, and of great importance to Allen's stone-quarrying business.*

It was earned by hard work, coupled with a workable and handsome design, and by taking a substantial risk.

A CHARITABLE COLLABORATION

Nash, Allen and Wood were all self-made men, and very different: Nash, the 'man of mode', obsessed with manners and correct behaviour; Allen, the entrepreneur, sober and efficient, and modest; and Wood, the eccentric, quarrelsome, obsessive visionary, who designed buildings of sublime beauty and originality. Their worlds were far apart, but they had a common interest in the city's prosperity. The Mineral Water Hospital was built as a result of their combined efforts.

While Nash worked tirelessly on the subscription list, Wood drew up the plans and directed the building works free of charge. As originally designed, the hospital was a fine pedimented building, its trapezoid plan following the angle of the streets to either side. Allen gave the stone as well as providing funding for the hospital. Nash was a Governor until his death, and Allen served a term as President in 1742. The reputation of all three men was much enhanced by their achievement in establishing the hospital.

PRIOR PARK

Ralph Allen was still determined to prove to the world the qualities of his Bath stone, and this he was to do triumphantly with Prior Park, the mansion he began building for himself close to his

BELOW *A watercolour of the Palladian Bridge at Prior Park by the artist T. E. Rosenberg. As John Wood related, there was a set 'perambulation for the curious', which was designed to show off the finer points of Prior Park and its grounds. The Palladian Bridge dates from 1750.*

Combe Down quarry in 1735. Wood's grand design, an adaptation of a Palladian villa, matched Allen's ambition. It was, in Philip Thicknesse's words, a 'noble seat, which sees all Bath and which was built, probably, for all Bath to see'; it would show the stone, described by Wood as 'neat, firm and dry', to its best advantage.

The porticoed main building was designed by Wood with curving galleries to either side and wings providing stables, storerooms and offices. Beside the proposed elevations of Prior Park in *The Description of Bath*, Wood illustrated, obviously with some pride, a square pavilion that was both a *porte-cochère*, under which coaches could stop and passengers alight in the dry, and a dovecote. Allen's pigeons were to be 'magnificently housed so that if a beautiful habitation is really an allurement . . . Mr Allen's pigeons will, in all probability, never desert their present abode'. But Wood, as frequently happened, fell out with his employer, and after ten years on the project he was forced to hand over to Allen's Clerk of Works Richard Jones.

Allen moved in to the house in 1741, before building work had finished. He was a generous host, and around him he assembled a number of talented writers, painters and actors. Henry Fielding was a frequent visitor, and he dedicated his novel *Amelia* to Allen. Squire Allworthy in *Tom Jones* is held to be a portrait of him:

> Neither Mr Allworthy's house nor his heart were shut against any part of mankind; but they were both more particularly open to men of merit. To say the truth, this was the only house in the kingdom where you were sure to gain a dinner by deserving it.
>
> Above all others, men of genius and learning shared the principal place in his favour; and in these he had much discernment; for though he had missed the advantage of a learned education, yet, being blessed with vast natural abilities, he had so well profited by a vigorous, though late application to letters, and by much conversation with men of eminence in this way, that he was himself a very competent judge in most kinds of literature.

The situation of the squire's house bore a resemblance to Prior Park, too. Water from a spring came 'tumbling in a natural fall over the broken and mossy stones till it came to the bottom of the rock':

> then running off in a pebly channel, that with many lesser falls winded along, till it fell into a lake at the foot of the hill,

BELOW *The poet Alexander Pope sketched in chalk at Prior Park by William Hoare. Pope was a frequent visitor, and one of his ideas for the gardens was to create the cascade in the wilderness area.*

ABOVE *The Circus, designed by John Wood, begun in 1754 and completed by his son, twenty-nine years after the original scheme for a circus 'for the Exhibition of Sports'. The watercolour is by Thomas Malton, 1784.*

about a quarter of a mile below the house on the south side, and which was seen from every room in the front. Out of this lake, which filled the centre of a beautiful plain, embellished with groupes of beeches and elms, and fed with sheep, issued a river, that for several miles was seen to meander through an amazing variety of meadows and woods.

The squire's grounds were laid out with admirable taste, 'owing less to Art than to Nature', in Fielding's words; and so they were at Prior Park.

The description in *Tom Jones* was published in 1749, a year before Richard Jones put up, halfway down the view from the house, a roofed bridge with pedimented end pavilions. It was similar to an earlier one at Wilton and based on an actual design by Palladio.

Alexander Pope was another frequent visitor to Prior Park, and he is thought to have contributed to the plan of the garden. Allen befriended him after the publication in 1743 of Pope's *Literary Correspondence*, which the author untruthfully claimed had appeared without his consent. Allen, with characteristic

BELOW *Details of the emblematic motifs carved on the metopes of the first-floor frieze on the Circus.*

benevolence, offered to help him, a deed immortalized in the lines from the Epilogue to Pope's *Satires*:

> Let humble Allen, with an awkward shame,
> Do good by stealth and blush to find it fame.

The actors David Garrick and James Quin were among Allen's guests, and the painters Thomas Gainsborough and William Hoare.

LATER URBAN SCHEMES

Between 1739 and 1748, while writing his book, Wood was busy with plans for the terraces of lodging houses now known as the North and South Parades. Then his thoughts turned once again to his original plans of 1725 for rebuilding the whole city on classical lines.

There was opposition to his plans for the Circus he wanted to build on the ground above Gay Street, and it was not until 1754 that Wood ceremonially laid the foundation stone. He was never to see this, the most monumental of his urban schemes, completed, as he died three months later – not yet fifty years old. It was left to his son to carry out his father's plans. The Circus was to bear little resemblance to the 'grand circus for the exhibition of Sports' of which Wood had dreamed, but it represents a fascinating synthesis of John Wood the Elder's interests and beliefs, formed during the course of his life.

In designing the Circus, Wood had in mind two ancient and very different sites: Stonehenge, not far away in Wiltshire, and the Colosseum in Rome. Wood had surveyed Stonehenge and published a book of his findings in 1747. The form and dimensions of the prehistoric circles at Stonehenge were initially known to Wood from Inigo Jones's book on the subject, which illustrates a circle 300 feet (91 metres) in diameter with three symmetric gaps – almost the exact configuration of the Circus.

The Colosseum Wood knew only from engravings, unlike Stonehenge, and it would have been hard for him to imagine the enormous size of this great elliptical amphitheatre adorned with three tiers of the Doric, Ionic and Corinthian orders. In any event, Wood had a habit of adapting information and facts to suit his own notions. He turned the Colosseum 'outside in', in Smollett's description, so the orders appear congested. Wood applied 648 closely packed columns to the outside of the thirty houses of the Circus.

Intriguing adornments to the architecture of the Circus are the 525 metopes on the first-floor frieze, consisting of snakes, winged hearts, helmets, dolphins, tortoises and crocodiles, among other features. They have always attracted curiosity as Wood's reasons for using some of them are obscure. One of his primary sources was a book published a century before, George Wither's *A Collection of Emblemes Ancient and Moderne*. Emblem books, which contained epigrammatic mottoes or verses accompanied by symbolic and allegorical woodcuts or engravings, had been a popular source for ornament since the end of the sixteenth century. They had many motifs in common with masonic emblematic imagery, and, since Wood was an enthusiastic freemason, this would undoubtedly have been part of the attraction for him. The large stone acorns around the top of the Circus are a reminder of King Bladud and the supposed origins of Bath. Wood's unexecuted plan was that there should be a large equestrian statue of George II in the middle of the Circus, where there are now trees.

Arthur Young, visiting Bath in 1768, wrote appreciatively, 'Believe me, *Bath* greatly exceeds *London* in regularity of building, and in being proportionately a much finer city.' It was the

ABOVE *An emblem from George Wither's book, published in 1635, which was the source of inspiration for the decorative metopes in the Circus. Part of the accompanying poem reads, 'Two Serpents (WISDOM'S EMBLEMS) twisted are . . .'*

ABOVE *The Doric and Ionic orders on the two lower storeys of the buildings in the Circus, which has, like the Colosseum, the Corinthian order above. The painter Thomas Gainsborough was one of the original residents of the Circus.*

Circus that caught his eye most particularly, and he judged its elegant character to lie 'somewhere between profusion and simplicity'.

JOHN WOOD THE YOUNGER

John Wood the Younger was indoctrinated with his father's ideas but did not have his vision. Orderly and possessed of a calm temperament, the son was, however, able to negotiate contracts and leases with ease and efficiency. When working together in Liverpool in the early 1750s, father and son were both made Freemen of the city, and in 1751 John Wood the Younger was elected a member of The Most Honourable & Facetious Society of Ugly Faces. To be eligible it was necessary to be a bachelor, a man of honour and of a facetious disposition; each member had to have 'something odd, remarkable, droll, or out of the way in his Phiz'. The younger Wood's qualifications for membership are recorded in architectural terms:

> A stone colour'd complexion, a dimple in his Attick Story.
> The Pillasters of his face fluted. Tortoise-ey'd, a prominent
> nose. Wild grin, and face altogether resembling a badger, and
> finer tho' smaller than Sir Christopher Wren or Inigo Jones's.

Wood married in the following year and so had to resign. In Wood's life of earnest endeavour, this is the only note of humour that was recorded.

The two Woods made an admirable partnership. John Wood the Elder designed the Circus and provided the inspiration for the Royal Crescent, but without his son it is probable that neither would have been built.

THE ROYAL CRESCENT

The conveyance of the land on which the Royal Crescent was built is dated 19–20 December 1766. It was granted by the ground landlord, Sir Benet Garrard, to John Wood and Thomas Brock, Wood's trustee, to whom he was related by marriage. On Thursday 21 May the *Bath Chronicle* noted:

on Tuesday last the foundation stone was laid of the first house of the intended new building above the Circus, called The Royal Crescent.

No. 1, the first house, was built for Thomas Brock and forms the eastern end of the Crescent. The building of the Crescent took eight years altogether, and it was to include some of the grandest houses in Bath; some were permanent homes and some were rented for the season. A number of the houses were built speculatively by groups of craftsmen who brought their different skills to each individual venture.

The Crescent is a great elliptical curve almost 50 feet (15 metres) high and 500 feet (152 metres) long. It comprises thirty terrace houses that are identical apart from a small variation to one. After the first six houses had been built, it was realized that to fill the proposed site Michael Hemmings, who in 1767 leased the plot of No. 7, would have to make a very slight correction to the curve. This is noticeable only in the roofline.

The design of the Crescent is one of restraint and balance; without the clutter and flamboyance of the Circus, it is an elegant understatement. The ground floor is severely simple, emphasizing the drama of the main feature of the Crescent: the giant Ionic order of 114 columns that are over 20 feet (6 metres) high; in the

ABOVE *The drawing room of No. 16 Royal Crescent at the front of the building. Fine marble mantelpieces such as this one were installed in many of the Georgian houses in Bath. The painting of George III is by Gainsborough Dupont, nephew of Thomas Gainsborough.*

manner of Palladio, the columns extend from the first to the second storey. There is a minimum of detail, with the base of the columns and the cornice as plain as the frames of the windows and doors. The end-pavilions are marked by paired columns, and the centre of the Crescent, No. 16, is marked by a single arched window between the paired columns.

Uniformity was throughout of the essence, and Wood wrote into the contract that the builder of each house in the Crescent should 'cleanse and tone down the stone work on the outside . . . to the end no crack should appear and the whole building may be of one colour.' Looking at the Crescent today, it is evident that this stipulation was observed.

On the approach to the Royal Crescent, Wood's carefully planned rise in the ground towards the end of Brock Street hides it until the last possible moment and heightens the astonishment felt as the Crescent comes into view. The harmony, economy and elegance are breathtaking, on the first and every subsequent visit. Royal Crescent is, indeed, the apogee of Bath architecture.

All the houses in the Crescent were built by 1774, and before that several persons of note had moved in. Christopher Anstey, author of *The New Bath Guide*, the humorous epistles of the Blunderhead family describing in verse their impressions of Bath, was living at No. 4; Philip Thicknesse, author of *The Valetudinarian's Bath Guide*, was living with his third wife at No. 9; and Thomas Linley, Director of the Bath concerts, was living with his family at No. 11. Four years after the Crescent was completed, Mrs Elizabeth Montagu, famous bluestocking and literary hostess, came to live at No. 16.

Mr Brock, who was the original occupier of No. 1, was seldom in Bath as he was Chester's town clerk. He died in 1786 and in that year Marie-Antoinette's lady-in-waiting, the Princesse de Lamballe, stayed in No. 1 with a large retinue that included her own physician. The French Revolution was to claim the lives of both the Princesse and her mistress. In 1796 Frederick Augustus, Duke of York, second son of George III and grandson of

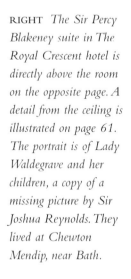

RIGHT *The Sir Percy Blakeney suite in The Royal Crescent hotel is directly above the room on the opposite page. A detail from the ceiling is illustrated on page 61. The portrait is of Lady Waldegrave and her children, a copy of a missing picture by Sir Joshua Reynolds. They lived at Chewton Mendip, near Bath.*

ABOVE *The Duke of York suite, named after 'The Grand Old Duke of York', brother of the Prince Regent, who occupied No. 16 Royal Crescent in 1797. The pastel portraits are the work of William Hoare, one of Bath's best-known painters of the Georgian period. This room has a magnificent plasterwork ceiling.*

Frederick, Prince of Wales, 'engaged the first house in the Crescent', and subsequently rented No. 16. Katherine Plymley recorded in her diary that the Duke paid the very large sum of £5,000 for No. 16, which was already elegantly furnished and had a coach house and stabling for sixteen horses. The lady of letters Hannah More was to write, 'their Highnesses of York are become almost inhabitants, and very sober and proper their behaviour'.

The Duke enjoyed Bath, and, contrary to the description, indulged in heavy gambling and womanizing. His recurring stomach problem 'was happily relieved in the winter by the Bath water'. He later became Commander-in-chief of the Army and is well known from the nursery rhyme:

> The Grand Old Duke of York
> He had ten thousand men
> He marched them up to the top of the hill
> And he marched them down again.

In the Duke of York's time the layout of No. 16, and some of the other houses in the Crescent, followed the standard eighteenth-century pattern for town houses. On the ground floor was a large and a small reception room. Most houses had no dining room at this date, and the smaller of the two rooms would have contained a gate-leg table that could be set up when required. At the rear of the house was a cantilevered stone staircase. On the first floor, the *piano nobile*, was the drawing room, occupying the full width of the building. To the drawing room the ladies would withdraw after dinner to drink tea. This was generally a light, feminine room, with walls of painted plaster, or hung with paper or fabric. Above the drawing room were the bedrooms and above them the much smaller servants' rooms in the garret.

In 1950, No. 16 ceased to be a private house and became a guest house. Twenty-one years later it was, with No. 15, redesignated a hotel, and in 1974 it was sold to a local doctor and a garage owner. When John Lewis and John Tham bought the hotel in 1978, it had forty-one bedrooms and six bathrooms. Apart from

BELOW *A view from the garden into the ground-floor room of No. 16 that was – and may still be – used for dining. The original furniture would have included a gate-leg table that could be set up when required. In the eighteenth century it was rare to find a room used solely as a dining room.*

the inadequate facilities, it was very run down. A headline in a local newspaper (making a reference to the television series featuring a shambolic hotel) read, 'Fawlty Towers changes hands'.

The architect William Bertram was asked to restore as far as possible the original splendour of No. 15 and No. 16. Most of the rooms had to be returned to their original dimensions, and damage to the plasterwork and decorative features repaired. Windows that were fitted with sliding sashes, of a type supposedly introduced in Bath in 1696, had been altered (perhaps in the belief once held that light contributed to health). These were returned to their original state, with glazing bars as shown in Thomas Malton's picture.

At the finish of the restoration there were twenty-nine bedrooms, all with bathrooms *en suite*. The result was a unique hotel, decorated in period style, and with appropriate furniture and eighteenth-century paintings and prints. Acclaim was quick to follow, and in 1980 The Royal Crescent hotel was given the Egon Ronay Hotel of the Year Gold Plate Award – one of the highest accolades.

The two houses have some very fine ceilings, of which that of the Percy Blakeney room on the first floor of No. 16 is an example. In the adjoining bedroom is a late seventeenth-century four-

ABOVE *A fine cantilevered stone staircase such as was installed in several of the houses in the Royal Crescent. This one is at the rear of No. 16. The bust of Plautilla, after the Antique, is by Prince Hoare, brother of the painter William Hoare.*

poster bed given to the hotel in the 1970s by Charles Robertson, author of *Bath: An Architectural Guide*, on the understanding that it would never leave the house. The suite is named after Sir Percy Blakeney, the Scarlet Pimpernel of Baroness Orczy's fiction, who, after his adventures in Revolutionary France, married and settled at No.16. Charles Dickens, Jane Austen and Henry Fielding are other writers who used the Royal Crescent in their novels.

The Duke of York suite spreads behind four windows on the first floor of the main façade of No. 15. The plasterwork ceiling of what was once the drawing room of the house is certainly one of the finest to survive in Bath. It is divided into geometric compartments, and is decorated with scrolling foliage, interlaced ribbons, acanthus leaves, trophies, musical instruments and birds of great elegance. The decorations were probably carried out by craftsmen from Bristol, where there was a strong tradition of fine-quality plasterwork. The various pattern-books then available were sources of inspiration for the design of decoration of this kind.

The contrast between the front elevation of the Royal Crescent and the backs of the houses could not be greater: a case of 'Queen Anne in front and Mary-Anne behind'. The form of the building behind as well as inside was a matter for each leaseholder in the

BELOW *The back elevations of the buildings in the Royal Crescent lack the symmetry of the front, and the quality of the finish varies greatly. Cut ashlar was used for some, as here at the back of No. 15 and No. 16, while for others rubble stone was used. This is the garden of the hotel.*

Crescent. They are a mixture and, in some cases, a muddle. The richer owners used cut ashlar to face the back of their houses and others used Bath rubble stone. The buildings across the garden at the back were originally coach houses and stables for the houses in the Crescent. The Villa and Pavilion in the gardens of No. 13 and No. 14 are small Palladian gems, the Villa designed by John Wood the Younger himself.

Next to these two buildings was a blank wall of no aesthetic or architectural merit. After discussions with the Bath City Planners, William Bertram's designs for the 'Dower House' to occupy this area were accepted, and between 1983 and 1986 they were carried out. In such a sensitive site the new building had to be in sympathy in scale and design with its eighteenth-century Grade I neighbours. The Dower House is not a Georgian pastiche but a late twentieth-century response to the precepts of classical archi-

ABOVE *Across the gardens at the back of the Royal Crescent are some fine examples of the classical architecture of the Georgian period. This is the Pavilion in the grounds of No. 14, which contains hotel suites named after two famous figures associated with the history of Bath: Beau Nash and Jane Austen.*

tecture. It stands in harmony with its neighbours and in 1986 won a Civic Trust award. The architect saw the discrete Crescent entrance to No.16 as a 'gatehouse' to the main building, and to a 'college' of buildings across the garden at the back that includes his worthy addition.

In 1987 The Royal Crescent hotel changed hands. When it came on the market again nine years later it was bought by Cliveden plc, the Chairman, John Lewis, and the Managing Director, John Tham, having in the meantime created the country's highest-rated hotel at Cliveden. The Royal Crescent had become much in need of refurbishment. Rupert Lord, the interior designer of Cliveden, was asked to redecorate The Royal Crescent hotel, and he chose the pale colours and Regency stripes of late eighteenth-century Bath as his starting-point for the redecoration. Historical sources for this period include T. H. Vanherman's *Every Man his own Painter* of 1829. Vanherman wrote:

> Lavender colour . . . lake, or rose pink, with a good
> portion of white (turned into peach blossom colour with
> the addition of a little Prussian blue) is an elegant tint for
> a drawing room.

'I wanted to echo the less fussy interiors of the Regency period,' said Rupert Lord; the period of 'immaculate white linen, polished leather boots, the sparkle of gold buttons on navy mohair coats. The Regency crispness of dress matched the crispness of their décor.' 'The house imposes a calm,' he said. 'There is a sense of luxury and lack of rush and bustle . . . I want people to feel they are coming to a house with all the graciousness of the Georgian period.' Not only the style of decoration but the style of living and entertaining reflects that of a former and more elegant age.

Through the acquisition of the original coach house to No. 18, there was now an opportunity to add to the 'college' of buildings in the garden. William Bertram and his partner Ted Brewster created within the shell of an eighteenth-century building a Bath House with the facilities of one in Japan, a country where bathing is a tradition. In a city that has for centuries been renowned for its baths, this is an appropriate addition.

As complete as at the time it was built, Royal Crescent is one of the eternal glories of Bath, its elliptical form as applied for the first time to terrace houses being one of John Wood the Younger's most important innovations. When Mrs Elizabeth Montagu was living at No. 16, she wrote of the 'threshold' of grass in the

ABOVE *A pen and wash drawing by Grimm, done from the window of a house in the Orange Grove in June 1789. Here he records the building of 'Pulteney Town' on the side of the river opposite the city centre. A barge bringing stone from the stoneyards is moored alongside the site.*

foreground leading to the wide view over the city beyond, 'The beautiful situation of the Crescent cannot be understood by any comparison with anything in any town whatsoever.'

THE RAGE FOR BUILDING

Smollett's reactionary squire, Matthew Bramble, who described the Circus to the fictional Dr Lewis as 'a pretty bauble, contrived for shew', made a reference to the projected Crescent and continued:

> when that is finished, we shall probably have a Star; and those who are living thirty years hence may, perhaps, see all the signs of the Zodiac exhibited in architecture at Bath.

This was not to happen quite as he imagined, but there was a great explosion in building, which reached its peak in the 1770s.

This was after the three principal protagonists were gone: John Wood died in 1754, Beau Nash in 1761 and Ralph Allen in 1764.

Humphry Clinker was published in 1769, and here is Bramble's description of the city at that time:

> the rage of building has laid hold on such a number of adventurers that one sees new houses starting up in every outlet and every corner of Bath; contrived without judgement, executed without solidity, and stuck together, with so little regard to plan and propriety, that the different lines of the new rows and buildings interfere with, and intersect one another in every different angle of conjunction. They look like the wreck of streets and squares disjointed by an earthquake, which hath broken the ground into a variety of holes and hillocks; or, as if some Gothic devil had stuffed them altogether in a bag, and left them to stand higgledy piggledy, just as chance directed.

Another version comes from the pen of Fanny Burney, writing from a house in Queen Square in 1791:

> This city is so filled with Workmen, dust and lime, that you really want two pairs of eyes to walk about in it, – one for being put out, and the other to see with afterwards. But as I, however, have only one pair, which are pretty much dedicated to the first purpose, you cannot, in reason, expect from me a very distinct description of it. Bath seems now, rather a collection of small Towns, or of magnificent Villas, than one City. They are now building as if the World was just beginning, and this was the only spot on which its inhabitants could endure to reside. Nothing is secure from their architectural rage.

Such was the frequency of accidents among the building workers, falling from scaffolding and suffering injuries to limbs while moving the blocks of stone, that in 1788 the Casualty Hospital in Bath was founded.

The squire of *Humphry Clinker* expressed his fears about the slightness of the buildings and, ten years later, Mrs Elizabeth Montagu made a similar complaint about even the largest houses, in the Circus and the Crescent:

> On the outside it appears a good stone edifice; in the inside
> it is a nest of boxes, in which I should be stifled if the
> masonry were not so bad as to admit winds at many places.

The trouble stemmed from the fact that 'every upstart of fortune, harnessed in the trappings of the mode, presents himself at Bath', in the words of Smollett. There they could 'mingle with the princes, and nobles of the land':

> Thus the number of people and the number of houses con-
> tinue to increase; and this will ever be the case, till the streams
> that swell this irresistible torrent of folly and extravagance,
> shall either be exhausted, or turned into other channels, by
> incidents and events which I do not pretend to foresee.

THE UPPER TOWN

The development of the upper part of the town became possible in the 1760s with the building of Milsom Street, which provided the connecting route to the land north of George Street and the Circus. Milsom Street was developed by Daniel Milsom, a wine cooper with a taste for building development. Initially the area was blighted by the uncomfortable presence of the Poor House, but this was eventually closed. During the period of the Regency, Milsom Street was to become Bath's grandest shopping street, and bow windows were inserted in some of the ground-floor lodgings.

In a few years the southern slopes of Landsdown were built over, but the disadvantage of living here was that the hub of social life was still in the region of the Abbey. The expense and discomfort of journeys up and down hill by sedan chair started residents thinking about building a place for entertainments closer to the new houses. Of the two existing Assembly Rooms, Wiltshire's was already too small, and the balls at Simpson's were crowded and uncomfortable.

A group of residents formed a tontine subscription, a system popular at the time for raising a loan: as each of the original subscribers died, their share was added to that of the survivors until the last survivor inherited all. It was in John Wood the

Younger's house in Brock Street that the shareholders met to set up the scheme. The first site they considered fell through, but Wood used this to his advantage and built Queen's Parade on the land. Robert Adam was invited to submit designs for a building on the site that was eventually chosen, but his designs were rejected on the grounds that they were too elaborate and thus too expensive. Wood's scheme, which was a version of Adam's plan, met with approval, and the foundation stone was laid in 1769. Two years later the project was completed, at a cost of £20,000.

The exterior design for the new Assembly Rooms, or Upper Rooms as they were called, was simple and unadorned, but the interiors were spacious and grand, and an immediate success. They comprised initially a ballroom, a tea room and an octagonal card room. In 1777 a new card room was added at the back of the building.

Within about two decades of the first stones of Brock Street being laid by John Wood's men, the Upper Town was virtually complete. Camden Crescent, designed by the eccentric John Eveleigh and begun in 1788, was to rival the Royal Crescent in

BELOW Pulteney Bridge, designed by Robert Adam at the height of his career. With shops on both sides of the bridge, and the road running between them, it is one of the city's most famous sights. The watercolour was painted in 1785 by Thomas Malton. Aquatints of his views were published for the visitors.

the quality of its architecture and its superb hillside position. However, the ground was unstable and began to slip, so the eastern part was never completed. The other fine crescent in the Upper Town, Lansdown Crescent, was designed by John Palmer and built between 1789 and 1793. The site was steep and uneven, and his solution was to create an undulating curve.

BATHWICK AND THE PULTENEYS

Another area of Bath ripe for expansion and development was the Bathwick estate, which lay across the river from the Abbey. This land came into the hands of William Johnstone, who

BELOW Portrait of Henrietta Pulteney at the age of eleven, by Angelica Kauffman. Her father was described as 'the richest commoner in England'.

ABOVE *The Sydney Hotel, a print after Nattes. Behind the hotel (now the Holburne Museum) lay the Sydney Gardens Vauxhall, as they were first known. During the summer season there were gala nights with fireworks, music and illuminations. Features of the gardens were a labyrinth, grotto, ruined castle, bowling greens and swings.*

changed his surname to that of his wife, Frances Pulteney, heiress to a considerable fortune. In 1764 Frances's cousin, William Pulteney, lst Earl of Bath, died, and the estate was left to her. To create a link between Bathwick and the main part of the city, the river had to be bridged. Pulteney gave the commission to his friend Robert Adam, and the building of Pulteney Bridge was begun in 1769; it was completed in 1774. His daughter Henrietta Laura had by now become one of the richest girls in England and was eventually, through her mother, to succeed to the title as Countess of Bath.

Henrietta turned to Thomas Baldwin to produce a scheme for Bathwick. Adam had been asked by her father to provide a plan, and Baldwin used Adam's idea of a wide street leading from the Pulteney Bridge across the estate. Work began in 1788, and Argyle Street, Henrietta Street, Great Pulteney Street and Laura Place were quickly built. Problems abroad brought the project to a halt. The French Revolution caused panic, with banks and builders, including Baldwin, going bankrupt. At the end of Great Pulteney Street, Baldwin was hoping to create a hexagonal garden surrounded by terraces of houses with a hotel facing up the long street. He was only able to build one terrace, which became Sydney Place, before being overtaken by events.

Harcourt Masters took over the scheme, and Sydney Gardens became a popular place of recreation. The Sydney Hotel was redesigned by Masters and sat imposingly at the end of Great

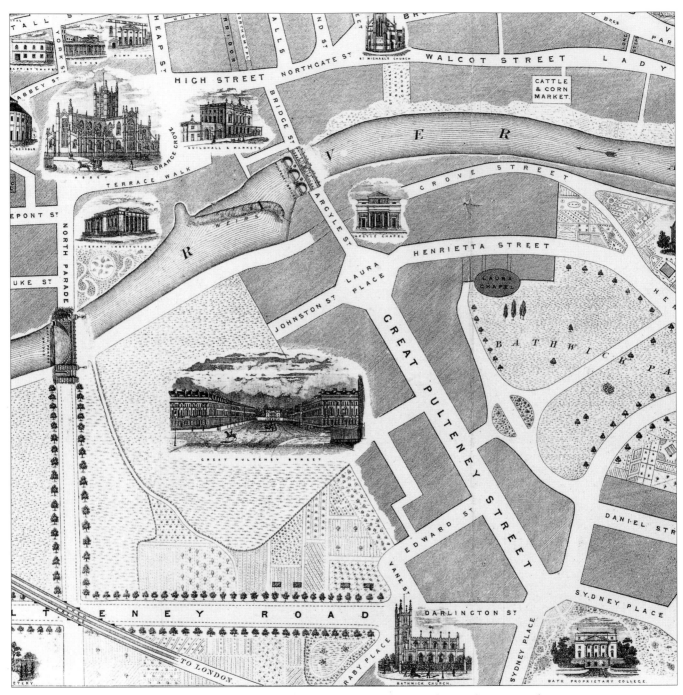

ABOVE *A Victorian map of Bath showing the development of the Pulteney estate across the river from the Abbey and Assembly Rooms.*

Pulteney Street. After the French Revolution, the Sydney Hotel became the home of the French monarchy in exile.

THE NEW PUBLIC BUILDINGS

Baldwin had designed the Guildhall in 1766, and the period between then and the date of his bankruptcy seventeen years later was one of great activity. In his position as City Surveyor, he was asked to improve the bathing facilities. This large-scale development involved the rebuilding of the Cross Bath, the provision of new Private Baths and the reconstruction of the Pump Room, as well as a design for the area between the baths. His plans were approved in 1788. John Wood the Younger had been asked to reconstruct the Hot Bath in 1775 (his only civic commission in Bath), and he designed an octagonal bath, open to the sky and surrounded by a series of small baths and dressing rooms. This was an incomplete solution, and it was left to Baldwin to produce the grand plan for the area.

In 1786 Baldwin had designed the colonnade to the north of the Pump Room. On the south side the colonnade led through to an entrance to the new Private Baths and to the King's and Queen's Baths. Between the colonnades rose the new west front of the Pump Room, which was completed by Palmer; to the west lay the Cross Bath. To provide access to the Pump Room, he created a street with a colonnaded pavement on both sides opening out at either end into an elegant segmented curve. Visitors could now arrive at the Pump Room under cover.

Fanny Burney wrote of Bath in 1791:

> It is beautiful and wonderful throughout. The hills are
> built up and down, and the vales so stocked with streets
> and houses, that, in some places from the ground floor on
> one side of the street, you cross over to the attic of your
> opposite neighbour. The white stone, where clean, has a
> beautiful effect, and even where worn, a grand one . . . in
> brief, yet in truth, it looks a city of Palaces, a town of hills
> and a hill of towns.

As the eighteenth century drew to a close, so too did the great period of building in Bath. In the course of the eighteenth century Bath had become, and remains to this day, the quintessential Georgian city.

THE AMUSEMENTS
OF BATH

DURING BEAU NASH'S TIME as Master of Ceremonies the atmosphere of the city changed. In former times Bath was a resort for cripples, wrote Daniel Defoe, but now it had become a resort of the sound as well as the sick; 'and a Place that helps the Indolent and the Gay to commit that worst of Murders, the killing of Time.' Miss Lydia Melford in Smollett's *Humphry Clinker* saw things differently: 'All is gaiety, good humour, and diversion,' she declared.

Right up until the end of the century, from the setting up of the first Pump Room in 1706 to the opening of the new room overlooking the King's Bath in 1795, the amenities of the city were being improved to reflect the emphasis on public entertainment: from morning until night, the company mingled and flirted, exchanged gossip and scandal, and discussed fashions and attachments.

Christopher Anstey described the pleasures to be found at Bath in his satirical letters in verse, supposedly written by different members of the Blunderhead family:

> At Bath, I'm arrived—and freely declare
> I do nothing but wonder, ask questions, and stare:
> Here's music, warm-bathing, fine dancing, and singing,
> With racketing, rioting, gaming and ringing;
> Such bustling and jostling, such hurries are made,
> At the pump-room, the ball-rooms, the play, and parade,
> You could swear 'twas a fair, or a race, or a show,
> With a constant succession of puppets a-row;

LEFT *A portrait of Christopher Anstey by John Raphael Smith. 'Mr Anstey, I cannot doubt, must sometimes be very agreeable; he could not else have written so excellent, so diverting, so original a satire,' wrote Fanny Burney of the author of* The New Bath Guide.

All dress'd so profusely, you'd think their resort,
Instead of such places, was hourly to Court;
Such a brilliant appearance of plenty and wealth,
That nothing seems wanted – but Virtue and Health.

The New Bath Guide, published in 1766, was read with great amusement by every visitor to the city. Even Horace Walpole, normally a sour critic, was enthusiastic in praise of Anstey's work:

What pleasure you have to come! There is a new thing
published that will make you bepiss [*sic*] your cheeks with
laughing. It is called the New Bath Guide . . . So much
wit, so much humour, fun and poetry, so much originality,
never met together before.

After the sensational success of the book – so successful that the publisher, Dodsley, after ten editions restored the copyright to the author, saying that no other book had paid so well – Anstey came to live in a house in the newly-built Royal Crescent and was much lionized by the *beau monde*.

ROYAL VISITORS

The visits of royalty never failed to create excitement, and Princess Amelia became, upon her first visit in 1728 at the age of seventeen, Bath's favourite royal personage. She arrived in the city by sedan chair. For her birthday, an ox was roasted, Morris dances were performed and guns fired, and there was a display of fireworks. It was during this visit that she requested that a dance should be allowed to continue after the official closing time, a request that was refused her by the King of Bath.

Princess Amelia came to Bath on several occasions, for amusement rather than to take the cure. In 1734 Mary Chandler was presented to her and humbly inscribed her poem, 'A Description of Bath', to the princess, hoping that 'Great Amelia's Name' would increase sales and defend her fame. By 1752 the charms of youth had deserted the princess, and she was hard of hearing, but she was described as 'affable and civil'. She 'drank beer like a fast young buck of the present day and took snuff like an old woman of her own day'. At noon and evening she was frequently to be found at the gaming table, playing Commerce; her language was emphatic without being vulgar and not quite '*comme il faut*'. Out

BELOW A Group at Bath, *a satirical print by S. R. Cruikshank dated 1796. It is based on a scene from Charles Macklin's play* The Man of the World, *set in Bath, and shows a duchess and a pin-maker's wife, among others, quarrelling over a game of whist.*

riding, which was one of her pleasures, she wore a hunting cap and a laced scarlet coat, and rode at a spanking pace, accompanied by her favourite groom Spurrier. She also amused herself for a few hours almost every day:

> in angling in the river, in a summer-house by the riverside in the garden formerly known by the name of Harrison's Walks, which has two fire-places in it, and to secure her against cold, puts on a riding habit, and a black velvet postillion-cap, tied under her chin.

BELOW Waiting for the Bath Coach, *the scene painted in watercolours by John Nixon in 1807. A London merchant and amateur artist who frequently visited his widowed sister-in-law in New King Street, Nixon was a keen observer of Bath life and characters.*

In November 1776 the princess paid another visit to Bath, causing Lady Diana Beauclerk to write to a friend:

> *Entre nous*, this is a most detestable place . . . and, to make it complete, the Princess Amelia is here, poking about it in every corner. It is impossible to stir without meeting her, and as I have no hopes of her being gracious enough to take notice of me, I am obliged to avoid her.

Princess Amelia's brother, Frederick, Prince of Wales, who died before he succeeded to the throne, came twice to Bath. His first visit was commemorated by Nash with the obelisk in Queen

Square, and on his second visit he was entertained by Ralph Allen, at Prior Park. The Prince of Orange, for whom Nash also erected an obelisk, in the grove that was named for him, came for a second time with his wife Princess Anne, sister of Princess Amelia and Frederick, Prince of Wales.

Two generations later, Frederick Augustus, Duke of York, came with his wife for the opening of the new Pump Room. He was presented with the Freedom of the City, but the ceremony did not go quite as planned for the mayor, Mr Palmer, found himself quite overwhelmed. 'I beg pardon but I am so impressed with your Royal Highnesses' presence that I cannot proceed,' he is reported to have said.

ABOVE *Bath clearly provided matrimonial opportunities. The presence of rogues and opportunists is gleefully satirized by Thomas Rowlandson in his print* The Successful Fortune Hunter, or Captain Sheldrake leading Miss Marrowfat to the Temple of Hymen.

THE COMPANY AT BATH

The *beau monde* came to Bath in the eighteenth century in the form of politicians, diplomats, men and women of letters and the givers of fashionable gatherings; and so, in the general tide of luxury, did every upstart of fortune. Matthew Bramble saw in the places of assembly and parading themselves in the city:

> Clerks and factors from the East Indies, loaded with the spoil of plundered provinces; planters, negro-drivers, and hucksters, from our American plantations, enriched they know not how; agents, commissaries, and contractors, who have fattened, in two successive wars, on the blood of the nation; usurers, brokers, and jobbers of every kind.

'Such is the composition of what is called the fashionable company at Bath,' wrote the disapproving character of Smollett's novel, that:

> a very considerable proportion of genteel people are lost in a mob of impudent plebeians, who have neither understanding nor judgment, nor the least idea of propriety and decorum; and seem to enjoy nothing so much as an opportunity of insulting their betters.

Bramble disliked, too, the noise, the tumult and the hurry, which was combined with ceremonial that had been imposed by Beau Nash and was more oppressive, in his opinion, than the etiquette of a German elector.

Jery Melford, another of Smollett's characters and sister of Lydia, revelled in the mixed company. Here a man had daily the opportunity of seeing people in their natural attitudes and true colours, 'descended from their pedestals, and divested of their formal draperies, indisguised by art and affectation':

> Here we have ministers of state, judges, generals, bishops, projectors, philosophers, wits, poets, players, *chemists, fiddlers, and buffoons.* If he makes any considerable stay in the place, he is sure of meeting with some particular friend, whom he did not expect to see; and to me there is nothing more agreeable than such casual rencounters. Another entertainment, peculiar to Bath, arises from the general mixture of all degrees assembled in our public rooms, without distinction of rank or fortune. This is what my uncle reprobates as a monstrous jumble of heterogeneous principles; a vile mob of noise and impertinence, without decency or subordination; but this chaos to me is a source of infinite amusement.

MORNINGS AT BATH

Days at Bath followed a regular pattern, beginning for the newly arrived with a visit from a doctor or an apothecary. Lady Luxborough, who established herself and her own servants at Mrs Hodgkinson's boarding house in Orange Grove in January 1752, was attended by the kindly Dr Oliver and the surgeon Peirce, who gave her every confidence that the nervous disorders and

LEFT *The Pumper at the Hot Wells prepares the glasses of water, a drawing by Grimm dated 1789. The rebuilding of the Hot Bath was the only commission that John Wood the Younger received from the Corporation, and it was completed in 1778.*

RIGHT *The new Pump Room in the 1790s, depicted by John Nixon. All manner of people paraded of a morning in the Pump Room, observing personalities and dress, and conversing.*

paralytic fingers from which she suffered would be much improved by drinking the waters and bathing. She usually drank the prescribed three glasses of the waters back at her lodgings, and she enjoyed the colour and animation of the scene at the baths.

'The amusement of bathing is immediately succeeded by a general assembly of people at the pump-house,' wrote Goldsmith, 'some for pleasure, and some to drink the hot waters.' The Pumper, with his wife and servant, stood behind a bar and dispensed the water in glasses of different sizes. 'The intervals between each glass of water are enlivened by the harmony of a small band of music, as well as by the conversation of the gay, the witty, or the forward,' wrote John Wood.

Teacakes, known after their maker as 'Sally Lunns', were supposed to have been eaten at the public breakfasts taken in the Assembly Rooms by people of fashion; others took breakfast in their lodgings. At the breakfast concerts, persons of rank and fortune were sometimes permitted to join in with the performers.

After 1752 the proceedings were watched over by a marble statue of Beau Nash, and before his death in 1761 by the Master of Ceremonies himself. A fine clock with a sundial was made, and given to the city, by Thomas Tompion, one of England's finest

clockmakers. It stood in the original Pump Room and, like the
statue, was moved to the new room before it was opened by the
Duchess of York in 1795.

After breakfast, on weekdays, some of the visitors made their
way to church. The Abbey was conveniently close to the Pump
Room, but there persisted a fear of contagion from the frequent
burials. The walls and pillars inside the noble Gothic building were
gradually being covered with memorials to members of the
aristocracy and landed gentry from all parts of the kingdom, sea
captains, merchants, politicians and others who had died at Bath
and for whom the cure had failed. Conspicuous among them was
a marble pyramid erected in memory of Ralph Allen's friend
James Quin with, beneath a medallion bearing a half-length figure
of the facetious actor, an inscription written by David Garrick:

> That tongue which set the table on a roar,
> And charm'd the publick ear, is heard no more;
> Clos'd are those eyes, the harbingers of wit,
> Which spake, before the tongue, what Shakespeare writ;
> Cold is that hand, which living was strech'd forth,
> At friendship's call, to succour modest worth.
> Here lies James Quin; – Deign, reader, to be taught,
> Whate'er thy strength of body, force of thought,
> In nature's happiest mould however cast,
> 'To this complexion thou must come at last'.

The secular tone of the epitaph accords with descriptions of
services in the Abbey, during which *billets-doux* and admiring
glances between members of the congregation were exchanged,
and there was little evidence of devotion. Visiting clergy were
frequently invited to preach, and there was the usual criticism of

the length and lack of interest of the sermons – and of the singing, from a correspondent to the *Bath Herald*:

> PERMIT me . . . to express my regret that more attention is not paid to the Musical Part of Divine Service in The Abbey Church . . . where, instead of those elevated Strains which inspire Devotion, the mind is fatigued by a dull Monotony disgusting to the musical ear.

BELOW *August 1790 saw the completion of the spire of St Swithin Walcot, one of several new churches and chapels built to accommodate the growing population. Inside there is a memorial tablet to Fanny Burney, and both Jane Austen's father and Christopher Anstey were buried here in 1805.*

Pews were reserved for those who paid rent for them and, eventually, the shortage of pews caused a number of churches to be built or refurbished – the domed St Michael's (rebuilt in the nineteenth century), St James's in Stall Street and Walcot Church. These were frequented more by the residents of Bath than by fashionable visitors. The preference of the visitors was for the six proprietary chapels, where rent from the pews lined the proprietors' pockets. The first of these was St Mary's Chapel (destroyed in the nineteenth century), built by the elder John Wood in 1734 exclusively for the use of the tenants of Queen Square.

A lady from Shropshire wrote in 1796 that she went to St Mary's on one of her Sundays in Bath, where she was:

ABOVE *One of John Nixon's watercolour sketches of Bath visitors: Mr Monteath of Dumfries reading the newspaper at Bull's Library in 1796. After the morning service, some of the company would repair to the libraries and booksellers' shops.*

accommodated with seats by Mrs Key, an old lady of large fortune in Queen's Square, who has a large front seat in the gallery and one for her servants behind her ...There is no Organ in this chapel, but it is very neat, very well warmed, as the chapels all are here, & the service is decently perform'd.

In the evening she went to prayers at the Octagon Proprietary Chapel in Milsom Street. This was advertised as 'the only safe place to worship in Bath, with no risk to health as there are no steps to climb and no bodies buried below'. Parson Woodforde doubted the decency of a chapel that had a fireplace on either side of the altar.

Her account continues with a reference to Christ Church, Montpelier, 'where the poor & strangers may worship the Almighty'. The idea for the church was said to have originated with William Wilberforce, who was shocked to find the poor entirely excluded from the Octagon and that there was too little room for them elsewhere. For visitors there were only the two seats in St James's for which no fee was demanded.

Charles Wesley said that preaching at Bath was like 'attacking the Devil in his own headquarters'. On his third visit he was confronted by Nash, who was fearful of the effect Wesley's Methodism might have on his own position as Master of Ceremonies, and on the gambling, dancing and other amusements that brought visitors and sustained the economy of the city.

A 1774 homily addressed to the shopkeepers, as well as the organizers of the public entertainments, railed against the vices of carrying on their businesses on Sundays:

> You, Gentlemen, cannot plead Necessity ... in keeping open your Publick Rooms on the LORD'S Day for the Sale of Tea and Cakes ... because the Command to keep holy the Sabbath Day is of universal Obligation on all Christians, high or low, rich or poor ... And may we not bear our Testimony against the Inhabitants of this licentious city ..? Do not many of them keep their Shops open on this Day and expose their Wares to Sale? And that not so much for the Supply of the Necessaries of Life, as the Luxuries and Superfluities of it? Add to this, the Multitude of Hair-dressers that swarm in the Streets, for the gratifying [of] the unnecessary Demands made by Pride and Vanity on that

Sacred Time, which ought to be employed to a better
Purpose, viz. the assembling ourselves in the House of God.

Selina, Countess of Huntingdon, attracted a number of famous people, including the Duchess of Marlborough and Lord Chesterfield, Lord Chatham and Horace Walpole, to the meetings of her own Calvinistic Methodist sect known as the 'Countess of Huntingdon's Connexion'. She was single-minded in her determination to revive the moral and religious life of the circle to which she belonged, and the chapel she built in 1765 was filled on Sundays to hear John Wesley and George Whitefield, among others, preach. John Penrose described the ticket given to his wife for a service on 16 March 1766: 'Strait is the Gate and narrow is the Way which leadeth unto Life and few there be that find it. Mat. 7. 14. This Ticket admits the Bearer to a seat in my Chapel. S. Huntingdon.'

COFFEE HOUSES AND EATING HOUSES

Mrs Elizabeth Montagu, 'Queen of the Blues', wrote to the Duchess of Portland in 1740:

> The morning after I arrived, I went to the Ladies' Coffee House, where I heard of nothing but the rheumatism in the shoulder, the sciatica in the hip, and the gout in the toe. I began to fancy myself in the hospital or infirmary, I never saw such an assembly of disorders . . . I hear every day of people's pumping their arms or legs for the rheumatism, but the pumping for wit is one of the hardest and most fruitless

RIGHT *A lady taking tea, a silhouette by Charles Rosenberg. On his trade card he described himself as 'profile painter to their Majesties and Royal Family'. The time taken for a sitting was advertised as one minute, and the prices from £6 to a guinea. He also offered 'Likenesses for Rings, Lockets, Trinkets and Snuff Boxes'.*

Mons.ᵣ Barretti.
by Northcote.

ABOVE *Portrait of Giuseppe Baretti. The original was painted for the Thrale family by Sir Joshua Reynolds in 1774; this copy is by James Northcote. The defective sight of the sitter, who was tutor to the Thrales' children, was intended to convey his great intellect.*

labours in the world. I should be glad to send you some news, but all the news of the place would be like the bills of mortality, palsy, four; gout, six; fever, one. &c. &c. We hear nothing but Mr Such-a-one is not abroad to-day; Oh! no, says another, poor gentleman, he died to-day. Then another cries, my party was made for quadrille to-night, but one of the gentlemen has had a second stroke of the palsy, and cannot come out; there is no depending upon people, no body minds engagements. Indeed the only thing one can do to-day, we did not do the day before, is to die.

Gentlemen had their own separate establishments, to which they withdrew to read the newspapers or converse, 'with a freedom and ease not to be found' in London. One visitor to Bath, who spent at least two hours each evening in a coffee house, found companions to his liking in a set that included the Speaker of the House of Commons, the Dean of Exeter, Dr Rice Carleton, a landowner from Suffolk (or Sussex), the chaplain to the Duke of Montagu and a 'knight of the shire' from Northamptonshire. They apparently spent some time with one another and formed 'a sort of society'. Friendships such as this, and even romantic attachments, were often discarded once the season was past.

Both ladies and gentlemen found their way to Mr Gill's, the pastry cook's, where Smollett's Lydia Melford treated herself to 'a jelly, a tart, or a small bason of vermicelli'. Gill was immortalized in Anstey's verses:

> Of all the Cooks the World can boast,
>   However great their skill,
> To bake, or fry, to boil, or roast,
>   There's none like Master GILL . . .
>
> O taste this Soup, for which the Fair,
>   When hungry, cold, and chill,
> Forsake the Circus and the Square
>   To eat with Master GILL . . .

Your Bard has liv'd at Bath so long,
 He dreads to see your bill—
Instead of Cash accept this Song,
 My worthy Master GILL.

BOOKSELLERS' SHOPS AND READING ROOMS

In these 'charming places of resort', as Lydia Melford described the booksellers' shops:

> we read novels, plays, pamphlets, and newspapers, for so
> small a subscription as a crown a quarter; and in these
> offices of intelligence, as my brother calls them, all the
> reports of the day and all the private transactions of the
> Bath, are first entered and discussed.

The Earl of Orrery wrote, 'flying from the Centre of all polite Conversation, the Pump Room, to the Asylum of all polite Literature, I entered the Palatinate of Mr Leake, the Bookseller':

BELOW *A circulating library depicted by Isaac Cruikshank. At Mill's library in Kingsmead Square, 'books [were] lent to read at 10s 6d per year, 3s per quarter, 1s 6d per month or by the single volume'. He also offered for sale quills, slates, pens, wax, paper, sand, message-cards, letter-cases and inkstands, as well as almanacks and Bibles.*

ABOVE *An engraving of the* Original Bath Mail Coach*, 1784, which was developed by John Palmer. His coach replaced the slow single-horse cart with one driver and thus speeded up delivery of the mail.*

This Leake is a most extraordinary Person. He is the Prince of the coxcomical Fraternity of Booksellers: and, not having any learning himself, He seems resolved to sell it as dear as possible to Others. He looks upon every Man, distinguished by any Title, not only as his Friend, but his companion, and he treats him accordingly; but he disposes of his Favours and Regards, as methodically as Nash takes out the ladies to dance, and therefore speaks not to a Marquess whilst a Duke is in the Room. As yet he is ignorant that my Earldom lies in Ireland, and to keep him so, I have borrowed the only Book of Heraldry he has in his Shop: by this method I shall be served many degrees above my Place, and may have a Squeeze of his Hand in presence of an Earl of Great Britain.

He went on to describe Mr Leake's shop, which was filled from the cornice to the skirting with books. He observed that 'the binding of his Books did not make so glittering a Figure as might be expected from the Library of a Person as illustrious as Himself.' Leake owned that his observation was right, and added that 'Some Fellows whose Ancestors, he believed, were Snails, had been daily expected from London, to illuminate and glorify his Museum.' In response to this, the Irish wag told him that he had no doubt that he would 'shew the Elasticity of his Genius, and the Nicknackatory of his Understanding by binding Lord Bacon in Hog's Skin, Bishop Sprat in Fish Skin and Cardinal du Bois in Wood'. Leake seemed delighted with the suggestion.

In the reading rooms and coffee houses were to be found the newspapers and pens, ink and paper, and it was here that many people came to write letters. These were addressed to friends and members of the family at home, eager to hear of the most recent happenings in this most fashionable of watering places, and to the men of affairs who had been left in charge of estates and business matters in the absence of their employers.

The mail originally travelled in a slow, single-horse cart with only one driver, and he was frequently attacked and robbed by highwaymen. The postal service was considerably improved after John Palmer persuaded the Government to introduce faster coaches with more than one driver specifically to carry mail, and a new system of relays. Added to this, the highways were constantly being improved. On 12 August 1784 it was reported in the *Bath Chronicle*:

> The New Mail Coach has travelled with an expedition
> that has been really astonishing, having seldom exceeded
> thirteen hours in going to or returning from London. It is
> made very light, carries four passengers, and runs with a
> pair of horses, which are changed every six or eight miles;
> and as the bags at the different offices on the road are made
> up against its arrival, there is not the least delay. The Guard
> rides with the Coachman on the box and the mail is
> deposited in the boot. By this means, the inhabitants of this
> city and of Bristol have the London letters a day earlier
> than usual, – a matter of great convenience to all, and of
> much importance to merchants and traders.

The scene outside the Post Office was all bustle and expectation as the coaches arrived and departed, to London, Bristol and Exeter, loaded with passengers as well as parcels, for it was with the mail coaches that some chose to travel to and from Bath.

A Tour of the Shops

Visiting the shops was a pleasurable and a necessary occupation for the lady of fashion. Lady Luxborough wrote of calling at Hayward's Tea Ware-House in Westgate Street, supplier to the nobility and gentry of 'All Sorts of Sugars, Teas, Coffee and Chocolate'. She went to Leake's bookshop and afterwards to the milliner's.

Millinery was the trade practised by Mary Chandler, hence she was known as the 'Milliner Poet'. The daughter of a Presbyterian minister, she had, at the age of eighteen, started a millinery business in the Abbey churchyard, directly opposite the Pump Room, where she specialized in Bath lace. The story is told that when she was fifty-four an old gentleman, unknown to her, came into her shop, bought a pair of gloves and proposed marriage. She thought the offer over and rejected it, explaining, 'To suppose a man can be a lover at sixty is to expect May fruits in December.'

On her morning walks through the city in 1752 Lady Luxborough would call in on the toymen. She was looking for trinkets to take home as presents, and she would have been shown by the dealers in fancy goods such trifles as an antique coin, a toothpick case, a locket or a hair ring of a type for which Bath was famous. She visited James Beresford, jeweller and goldsmith, in the Market Place. The Abbé Prévost remarked wisely that the dealers in jewels, delicacies and gallantries took advantage of 'a kind of enchantment which blinds every one in these realms of enjoyment to sell for their weight in gold trifles one is ashamed of having bought after leaving the place'. Lady Luxborough went also to see James and Peter Ferry, silk weavers of London and Bath, and John Graham, who sold 'Lawns, Cambricks, Velvets' as well as lace.

At about that time Francis Bennett, at the Star, was a purveyor of a multitude of wares, from haberdashery and household linen to groceries, snuff and cards. He also undertook the direction of funerals – a lucrative business in this resort of the frail and feeble – providing palls and cloaks and other necessaries as decent and cheap as in London. Later in the century there appeared in the *Bath Chronicle* a description

ABOVE AND BELOW RIGHT *Trade cards for two Bath shops. Carefully engraved on paper, these announcements were intended to list and advertise the goods and specialities of the business. Accounts were often written below, detailing and costing the customer's purchases.*

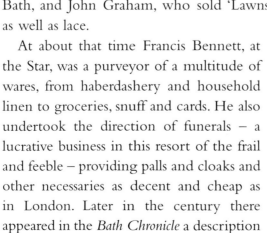

ABOVE *A coloured aquatint of Milsom Street, from* Bath, illustrated by a series of Views, from the drawings of John Claude Nattes*, which was published in 1806. It shows the bow windows of shops in the newly-fashionable shopping street.*

of the fancy goods to be found at Moore's Universal Toy-shop: fans of the types known as Mulbrowk, Cestuses, Balloon and Gibraltar, Paris crimping irons, 'combs that will not split', scissors; and, for gentlemen, toupee irons, silk bags and hair powder, concave razors of recent invention and card purses with Bath mottoes. Moore assured customers that his vegetable wash-ball, which prevented the face and hands from chapping, removed freckles and whitened the skin, was of 'superior quality to any ball yet sold in this kingdom'.

Ladies with time on their hands went in search of essences: amber, musk and bergamot. In short, in Bath were to be found all that they could desire:

> Painted Lawns, and chequer'd Shades,
> Crape, that's worn by love-lorn Maids,
> Water'd Tabbies, flow'r'd Brocades;
> Vi'lets, Pinks, Italian Posies,
> Myrtles, Jessamin, and Roses,

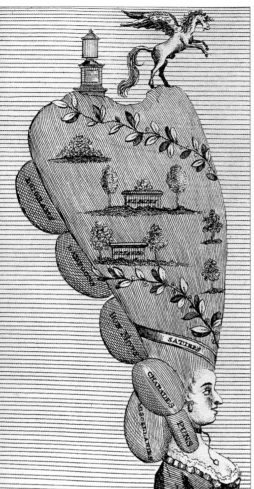

Aprons, Caps, and 'Kerchiefs clean,
Straw-built Hats, and Bonnets green,
Catgut, Gauzes, Tippets, Ruffs,
Fans and Hoods, and feather'd Muffs,
Stomachers, and Parisnets,
Ear-Rings, Necklaces, Aigrets,
Fringes, Blonds. and Mignionets;
Fine Vermillion for the Cheek,
Velvet Patches a *la Grecque*.

In so fashionable a resort it was important to be *à la mode* in matters of appearance and dress. *The Register of Folly* made mock of some of the more absurd fashions and practices:

For the Ladies at Bath make no more of their faces
Than the painter who daubs o'er his wainscots and bases;
And after three coats they have laid on, or more,
For beauties they'll pass, tho' no beauties before;
And their heads! (gracious heav'n!) 'tis true what I say,
You'd take them in meadows for cocks of new hay,
Which, expos'd in a tempest of boisterous weather,
Would twist them about in a whirlwind together.

In 1766 there was a vogue for a 'Minute Dress' and 'Two-minute Dress', so-named because of the time required to put them on. At the same date it became fashionable to wear spectacles and affect a degree of myopia.

ABOVE *The elaborate hair fashions of the late 1770s are satirized by Matthew Darly in his print of Lady Miller, which he entitled* Mount Parnasus or the Bath Sapho. *She published the results of her poetry competitions, excusing the poems' quality as 'they originated amidst the hurry of plays, balls, public breakfasts, and concerts'.*

EDUCATION AND ACCOMPLISHMENT

People of fashion might choose to attend public breakfasts at the Assembly Rooms and, when so disposed:

attend lectures upon the arts and sciences, which are
frequently taught there in a pretty superficial manner, so
as not to teize [*sic*] the understanding, while they afford
the imagination some amusement.

Lady Miller entertained those of a would-be literary disposition at *soirées* held at her villa at Batheaston, just outside the city. She devised a poetry competition in which guests placed their rhyming contributions in a vase brought back from Frascati and said to have belonged to Cicero. The gatherings represented the height of intellectual pretension. Fanny Burney described Lady

Eliza Lucas Work'd at Mrs Rosco's Boarding School Royal Crescent Bath in the year 1788

Miller as a 'round, plump, coarse looking dame', who seemed 'an ordinary woman in very common life, with fine clothes on', but despite her appearance and mock importance of manner, her Thursday evenings were well attended: 'nothing is more tonish than to visit Lady Miller, who is extremely curious in her company, admitting few people who are not of rank or fame'.

During the day, drawing masters and other teachers were to hand to help in the acquisition of proficiency in various artistic and sporting subjects. In 1783 it was reported in the *Bath Chronicle* that a subscription had been begun at a meeting of artists at the Three Tuns tavern, 'in conjunction with gentlemen who are lovers of the Arts', to establish an academy for study from Antique statues and the living model open to every class of artists, including amateurs.

Teachers of elocution, fencing and riding, dancing and music, offered their services by the hour; pianos and harpsichords were hired out by the week. Needlepoint pictures had their vogue, and in 1788 one Eliza Lucas stitched her most distinguished piece of work under the auspices of Mrs and Miss Rosco at their Academy in the Royal Crescent. At the time of the opening of the Academy the following entry appeared in the *Bath Chronicle*:

> Miss Rosco cannot find words and, if found, they would express the grateful sense she has of the favours and encouragement of her friends, begs leave to inform them, she opens her school in the Crescent on Monday 20th inst. Terms are as follows; Entrance £5. 5s. Board, washing, tea, French, writing, accounts, embroidery and all sorts of work, £30 per session. English grammatically taught, to which the utmost attention is paid by Miss Rosco – Only one vacation in a year, for six weeks, commencing a fortnight before Whitsuntide.

Although history does not relate which was the more successful of the two, Miss Rosco had a rival who also advertised in the *Bath Chronicle*. Miss Hudson, too, was eager to earn the attention of the fashionable folk:

> MISS HUDSON, Chapel-Court, Cross-Bath, takes the opportunity of acquainting the Nobility and Gentry, that she continues to teach that peculiar Art of EMBROIDERY, which was invented for the Queen's Bed, and which she has studied under the celebrated Mrs Wright. Also teaches to Embroider in Worsted, Chenilles, Ribbons &c.
>
> Of whom may be had, Sets of Materials, for Embroidery, with the most fashionable patterns for Screens and Pictures; Suits of Cloaths for Ladies, and Gentlemen's Waistcoats; Ladies' Habits, Work-Bags, &c, – MISS HUDSON also instructs Ladies to Draw and Paint from nature, upon the most reasonable terms; also to draw their own Designs for One Guinea.

WALKS AND JAUNTS

A general recommendation of the doctors was to take fresh air and moderate exercise. Bath was, as it is today, surrounded by hidden valleys and open downs. In fine weather the ways about the city were thronged with people on horseback, in carriages or on foot. In 1739 it was laid down that the sedan chairmen should convey invalids into the countryside, and away from the smoke and smell of the city, at the rate of sixpence for every half mile, so that they might benefit from the fresh air in fine weather. Local beauty spots, rural tea-gardens, country houses such as Prior Park: all were made the object of agreeable expeditions. Betsy Sheridan, towards the end of the eighteenth century, recorded in her journal for June:

> went to the Crescent Fields [below the Royal Crescent] which is the present Mall of Bath and I think the pleasantest I was ever in as one is literally walking in the fields with a most beautiful prospect all around at the same time that you meet all the company that is now here. There is something whimsical yet pleasing in seeing a number of well-dressed people walking in the same fields where Cows and Horses are grazing as quietly as if no such intruders came among them.

BELOW *A view of Bath from the series of prints after Nattes. The surrounding hills afforded walkers a fine panorama of the city, with the Abbey a conspicuous landmark.*

Horse racing was another form of diversion that took place in the open air – with the additional attraction of gambling among the onlookers. The *Bath Chronicle* reported:

> we find, that a very excellent Course is marked out on Lansdown for our Races, and that good sport is expected.

ABOVE *Bath Races, a detail showing the halt and lame descending the hill below the Royal Crescent. Rowlandson drew the scene several times, and this version was published as an aquatint in 1810.*

This alteration has long been wished for by the gentlemen who generally send their horses here, as they allow there is not a finer turf in the kingdom for running in all seasons, than that on Lansdown – whilst the Claverton course in dry weather, from being so near the rock, was very prejudicial to the horses; it is likewise much nearer and more convenient to the gentlemen of Bristol, Gloucestershire, &c. The continuance of the races is certainly of great consequence to the city, as it in some measure marks a commencement to our season and part of it's amusements, which for some years past have gradually been later and later, and it occasions the Theatre being opened a month sooner than otherwise it could possibly be.

BATH ASSEMBLIES

At the heart of fashionable life in Bath was the assembly, 'a general meeting of the polite persons of both sexes, for the sake of conversation, gallantry, news and play'. The Assembly Rooms were used for dancing and for the drinking of tea; the 'play' was mainly at cards, but games of shuttlecock and other forms of recreation also took place in the rooms.

A code of behaviour at public balls had been laid down by Nash, and these were adapted after his death in 1761 by the Masters of Ceremonies who succeeded him. Samuel Derrick, like his famous predecessor, insisted that standards in dress should be upheld:

No Lady can be permitted to dance Minuets, without a Lappet head [a style of headdress with a part that hung loose], and full-dress long Hoop, such as are permitted to dance Minuets at Court.

No Lady can be permitted to dance Country Dances with an Hoop of any kind; and those that chuse to pull their Hoops off, will always find a servant maid ready to assist them, and a proper Place to retire to for that purpose.

Every Gentleman chusing to dance Minuets, must present himself in a full Dress, or a French Frock Suit compleat, and a Bag wig.

Officers Regimentals are an Exception to this Rule, being every where proper; but every other kind of Lapel is improper for a minuet at Bath.

BELOW Country dancing at a Cotillion Ball at the New Assembly Rooms, *the original watercolour by Thomas Rowlandson for Plate X in* The Comforts of Bath *series. Katherine Plymley described both the Lower and New Assembly Rooms in her diary for 12 November 1796, and concluded, 'The new is undoubtedly much the most elegant.'*

ABOVE *Thomas
Gainsborough's imposing
portrait of Captain Wade
looks down from the
walls of the Octagon
in the new Assembly
Rooms. Wade was a
successor to Nash as
Master of Ceremonies in
1769 and was held in
much the same respect.*

It is recommended to the Gentlemen frequenting the Rooms
to remember that leather Breeches are by no means suitable
to the Decorum of the Place.

As before, stately minuets were danced at the beginning of a ball
and afterwards the country dances, for which the ladies were
required to remove the hoops from their dresses. The music ceased
at the stroke of eleven.

Between 1769 and 1777 the Master of Ceremonies was
Captain William Wade. He was the first to hold that position at
the New Assembly Rooms, which opened on 30 September
1771 with a *ridotto*, combining a dance with a concert. Wade's
'reign' is commemorated in the fine full-length portrait of him,
painted by Thomas Gainsborough for the Octagon, the original
Card Room attached to the Ballroom. The first Assembly
Rooms built by Harrison, and much extended, carried on and
were now known as the Lower Rooms; Wiltshire's, opposite it
in Terrace Walk, were closed.

In the Upper Rooms, as the new Assembly Rooms were
called, there was a Dress Ball on Monday evenings during the

season, a card assembly on Tuesday evenings, a concert on Wednesday evenings and a Fancy Ball on Thursdays. At a Monday evening ball in 1796 attended by Miss Plymley, the Duke and Duchess of York graced the company with their presence. The Duchess, in the opinion of the diarist, was wearing too much rouge, and so did all the ladies of her party. The Duke seemed good humoured and pleasant, but she did not like his countenance:

> They were both dressed in plain blue with the star. The
> Duchess's body & train was white spotted with gold,
> trimmed round the neck & down the sides with narrow
> black velvet studded with diamonds, her head dress a
> turban, diamond crescent, & large plume of feathers,
> diamond necklace and earrings.

No better place to observe the appearance of fashion was to be found than in the New Assembly Rooms, which on this occasion brought out 1,200 people.

GAMBLING AND GAMING

While men continue to be men, 'gaming will ever be the pleasure of the rich', wrote Goldsmith, for 'they fancy more happiness in being possessed of what they want, than they experience pleasure in the fruition of what they have'.

The ladies, too, were inveterate gamblers. Lady Mary Wortley Montagu wrote to her sister in 1725:

> The discreet and sober Lady Lechmere has lost such
> Furious summs at the Bath that 'tis question'd whether all
> the sweetness that the Waters can put into my Lord's blood
> can make him endure it, particularly £700 at one sitting.

Richard Steele, with his habitual irony, later wrote:

> I must own that I receive great pleasure in seeing my pretty
> countrywomen engaged in an amusement which puts them
> upon producing so many virtues. Hereby they acquire such a
> boldness as raises them near the lordly creature man.

Doctors even recommended gambling to their patients as a form of distraction.

It was as a professional gamester that Beau Nash first came to Bath, and in the end it was the third law against gambling, enacted in 1745, making it illegal to keep any 'house, room, or place, for

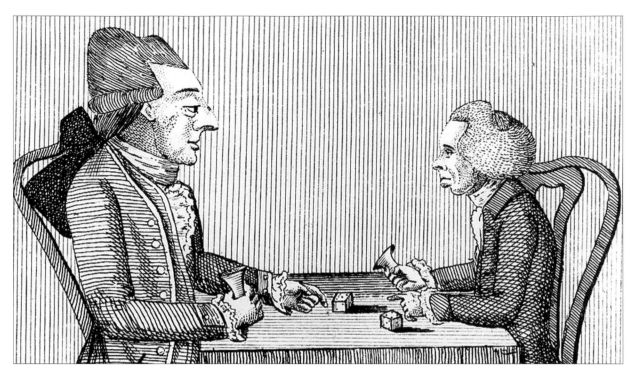

ABOVE *Gamblers at Bath, caricatured by Matthew Darly. After 1745 the fine for any person in Bath 'who shall play at, set at, stake or punt at' a proscribed list of card games was £50 ('except the Royal Palaces or where his Majesty, his heirs or successors shall then reside').*

playing', that reduced Nash to penury. Previously he had, as was eventually revealed, obtained a commission from the games of Hazard, Faro and EO played in the Rooms. Gambling continued after the laws were passed, but out of the public gaze, on cards, and on cock-fighting, boxing, horse-racing and other sports. Card games, not visibly played for a stake, were permitted in the Assembly Rooms every day except Sunday.

There were the winners and there were the losers, whose long faces were a feature of Bath. Philip Thicknesse in *The New Prose Bath Guide* warned:

> those who love Play must understand it in a *superlative degree*, if they expect to gain anything by it at Bath, where there are always *ingenious Men*, who live by their *great Talents* for *Play*; for however great and *Adept* a man may think himself at the Games of Whist, Billiards, etc., he will always find Men, and Women, too, here, who are greater and make it a Rule to divide the many Thousands lost every year at Bath *among themselves only*.

There were the tricksters, too, and events sometimes led to a violent quarrel, or a duel in which one or other of the contestants died. A man named Newman had his hand pinned to the table with a fork, his opponent remarking, 'Sir, if you have not a card hidden under that hand, I apologise.' Newman later committed suicide.

LEFT *Sarah Siddons in the role of Euphrasia in Arthur Murphy's tragedy* The Grecian Daughter, *a mezzotint after William Hamilton. Hazlitt was to write, 'Power was seated on her brow, passion emanated from her breast as from a shrine. She was tragedy personified . . . To have seen Mrs Siddons was an event in everyone's life.'*

THE THEATRE

The playhouse built at the time of Nash's arrival in Bath was evidently poorly attended. In 1737 it was closed and then sold, making way for the Mineral Water Hospital. The original idea for a new theatre in Orchard Street came from an actor called Hippisley and was taken up by John Palmer (father of the postal reformer). The theatre opened in 1750 and witnessed a series of theatrical triumphs before it was replaced by the Theatre Royal in Beaufort Street in 1805.

It was at the Orchard Street theatre in 1778 that Sarah Siddons made her début as Elvira in Sir John Vanbrugh's comedy *The Provoked Husband*. She had been dismissed from London's Drury Lane by David Garrick and had been seen at Birmingham by John

Henderson, who was at that time enjoying a considerable success acting at Bath, and recommended by him to Palmer. Mrs Siddons was to become the greatest tragic actress that England has ever known, and she did much to bring the genre of tragedy back into vogue.

In 1779 Garrick revised his opinion of her:

> I will venture to add a paragraph relative to our stage matters; and it is only to do justice to an excellent actress which has appeared here this season, a Mrs Siddons, who I really think is as much mistress of her business as any female I ever saw . . . and I declare my opinion of her to be all that my ideas can reach . . . Her Portia, Belvidera, and other pathetic parts in tragedy, are, I think, exquisitely fine.

Mrs Siddons left Bath in 1782, for the sake of her three children:

> . . . little magnets, whose influence draws
> Me from a point where every gentle breeze
> Wafted my bark to happiness and ease—
> Sends me adventurous on a larger main . . .

Those were her departing words as she led them to the front of the stage. She went back to London, and Drury Lane, where Richard Brinsley Sheridan had bought Garrick's share in the theatre.

The Bath Herald reported one of her triumphant return visits to Bath:

> It was not 'till Saturday night last, that Mrs SIDDONS was announced to appear a few nights at our Theatre – and at an early hour on Monday, there was not a seat unlet in any of the boxes for her performances. Her first character was the GRECIAN DAUGHTER: the avenues to the theatre were crowded at an early hour . . . to procure a sight of this unequalled Actress in a part which she had so often played on the same boards with, what was then thought, the summit of excellence and admiration.

ABOVE AND RIGHT
Pencil sketches by James Vertue of three Bath players in character for The Gamester, *a play by Edward Moore that was first performed at Drury Lane in February 1753.*

Sheridan's comedies were frequently played at the Orchard Street theatre and two are particularly associated with the city, *The Rivals*, the first of his plays and set in Bath, and *The School for Scandal*, originally entitled 'The Slanderers: A Pump Room Scene'. Sheridan's father had set himself up in Bath as a teacher of elocution, and the playwright had lived there as a young man

for long enough to gather an impression of the frivolity and
spitefulness of Bath society. Lady Sneerwell, Mrs Candour and
Sir Benjamin Backbite are names he gave to characters in *The
School for Scandal*, while in *The Rivals* he created the character of
Mrs Malaprop, who famously gave her name to the word
'malapropism'.

MUSIC, SCANDAL AND SCIENCE

Ever since Beau Nash had hired musicians to play for visitors to
the baths, concerts had been one of the principal diversions of the
city. The musicians performed in the Pump Room, in the
Assembly Rooms and during breakfasts in Spring Gardens; fine
organ playing and choral singing were to be heard in the Abbey.

For two decades the musical life of the city was dominated
by the figure of Thomas Linley. He was the director of music
at the Assembly Rooms, engaging the artists and conducting
performances; he was himself a composer and player of the
harpsichord; he brought the music of Handel back into favour;
and he was the father of musical prodigies.

Elizabeth Linley, the spirited eldest daughter of Thomas, was a
singer, and as beautiful as she was talented:

> The tone of her voice and expression, her manner of
> singing, were as enchanting as her countenance and

LEFT *A miniature of the singer Elizabeth Linley by Richard Cosway. Her talented family lived in Bath, and many fell in love with her, but it was Sheridan who won her hand. Cosway was part of the circle of artists and musicians that moved easily between Italy, London and Bath.*

conversation. In her singing, with mellifluous-toned voice, a perfect stroke and intonation, she was possessed of the double power of delighting an audience equally in pathetic strains and songs of brilliant execution, which is allowed to very few singers.

The Bishop of Meath said that 'She formed the connecting link between angel and woman', and Horace Walpole that 'Miss Linley's beauty is in the superlative degree. The King admires her and ogles her as much as he dares to do in so holy a place as an oratorio.'

Sheridan, like many others, fell in love with the seventeen-year-old Elizabeth, whose romantic history to date had been made famous by Samuel Foote's play *The Maid of Bath*, in which she is portrayed as Miss Linnet. Possessed of great charm, Sheridan immediately triumphed over his rivals and won her confidence. In the spring of 1772 the pair disappeared dramatically from Bath. Sheridan left a letter explaining that their abrupt departure had been necessary in order to free Elizabeth from the unwanted attentions of a certain Captain Mathews, a married man and a friend both of himself and of the Linley family. The runaway couple were next heard of in Lille. Elizabeth had found shelter in a convent, from which she was, a month later, retrieved by her father. In the interval Sheridan had declared his passion, and they had married in secret. Captain Mathews, meanwhile, had published a denial of Sheridan's accusations, labelling him a 'liar and treacherous scoundrel'.

Sheridan returned to England soon after Elizabeth and her father, and fought a duel with Mathews, who begged for his life and gave Sheridan a written apology. Bath society now ostracized Mathews for his cowardly behaviour, and he left the city. Soon, however, he returned demanding satisfaction from Sheridan, and a second duel was fought at Kingsdown, a hill close to Bath. This was a very bloody affair, ending with both men on the ground and Mathews stabbing Sheridan with his broken sword. Mathews emerged the winner, with Sheridan receiving the more serious wounds. He and Elizabeth were forcibly separated by their two fathers. She resumed her singing and at Oxford caused in the undergraduates 'a sort of contagious delirium'; Sheridan went to live in London. There, on 13 April 1773, they underwent a second marriage, and from that time onwards Elizabeth was forbidden by her husband from receiving payment for her performances. He insisted that they live by his writing and she as a gentlewoman.

An accomplished musician from Hanover who settled for a time in Bath was William Herschel. For sixteen years he worked as music master, organist at the Octagon Chapel and conductor of the orchestra at the Assembly Rooms. He was an enthusiastic amateur astronomer, and would rush home after evening performances to observe the night sky. He was determined 'to leave no spot of the heavens unexamined', and since he was unable to afford a telescope, he built one of his own. In 1781 he discovered a new planet, Uranus, and became the first astronomer since ancient days to make such a discovery. In the following year his brilliance was recognized. He was appointed court astronomer to George III and left Bath for London.

BELOW *A portrait of William Herschel by John Russell. Herschel had a successful career as a musician, composing, giving lessons and playing the oboe in Linley's Pump Room orchestra, until his interest in astronomy took over his life.*

As director of music at the Rooms came an Italian opera singer, Venanzio Rauzzini. He provided music of very high quality, but although a stirring musician, Rauzzini was no manager of money, and the concerts ran at a loss.

The tenor Michael Kelly recorded in his reminiscences a few agreeable days spent with his old friend and master Rauzzini. 'Everything at Pyramid [Perrymead] breathed content and happiness; professional people, of all descriptions, were welcome to his hospitable table':

> While we were staying with him, Madame Mara and Signora Storace were also his inmates, and every evening we had music of the best sort; Rauzzini himself presiding at the piano-forte, and singing occasionally. He had lost the soprano part of his voice, but his low contra alto tones were very fine, and his taste was exquisite, he was also a delightful composer.

In 1794 Haydn visited him at Perrymead.

At Bath Rauzzini was loved and respected by the residents and visitors, to some of whom he gave lessons. At his private performances musicians gave their services for nothing:

> I have known Mrs Billington [singer] renounce many profitable engagements in London, when Rauzzini has required the aid of her talents, and at her own expense, travel to Bath, and back to London, as fast as four horses could carry her, without accepting the most trifling remuneration. The singers at the King's theatre, Haymarket, were always allowed by the proprietors to give him their gratuitous assistance.

ABOVE AND BELOW LEFT Companion portrait drawings of the eccentric Philip Thicknesse and his wife Anne Ford by William Hoare. At this time the couple were living at No. 9 Royal Crescent. Anne Ford is depicted with her guitar, as in a Gainsborough portrait that Mrs Delaney found in such questionable taste.

PAINTERS AND SITTERS

The visitors, whether pursuing health or diversion, provided portrait painters with an almost constant flow of commissions. Of the

ABOVE *A self-portrait by Thomas Barker of Bath; behind him stands his patron Charles Spackman. One of Barker's favourite views was of Hampton Rocks, the site of old quarry-workings overlooking Bath and the Avon valley.*

artists at work in Bath, there were several, including Ozias Humphry, who painted miniatures. These small-scale likenesses needed almost no drying time and were particularly suited to the transitory Bath clientele.

Gainsborough was for a time the most sought-after of the painters of full-scale portraits. Encouraged by Philip Thicknesse to leave the quiet city of Ipswich for a more interesting and prosperous life, he took up residence in Bath in 1759. His circle of friends included Ralph Allen, the musical Linley family and the actors Henderson and Quin, all of whom sat to him.

People of fashion were frequent callers at his studio, among them Mrs Delaney, who wrote in a letter to her sister:

> This morning went with Lady Westmoreland to see Mr Gainsborough's pictures and they may well be called what Mr Webb unjustly says of Rubens – they are 'splendid impositions'. There I saw Miss Ford's picture – a whole length with her guitar, a most extraordinary figure, handsome and bold; but I should be sorry to have any one I loved set forth in such a manner.

The portrait was in the new grand style developed by Gainsborough for his sitters at Bath.

Anne Ford married Philip Thicknesse as his third wife and, in exchange for the promise of a portrait of her husband as a pendant to her own, she gave Gainsborough the guitar depicted in the portrait. Gainsborough worked on other portraits instead of finishing the one of Thicknesse, and this eventually led to a quarrel that contributed in 1774 to the painter's departure for London. Thicknesse, in his rage, described the unfinished picture as 'that scare-crow'.

Thicknesse was renowned for his quarrelsome nature, but companion drawings in chalk of him and his wife were completed without incident by William Hoare. Indeed, in his *New Prose Bath Guide* Thicknesse wrote of Hoare's talent for working in crayons and in oils, adding generously that 'when genius and moral character are united in the same man, he becomes doubly respectable'. Hoare's altarpiece *The Pool of Bethesda* for the Octagon Chapel, and his connection with the Mineral Water Hospital through the donation of his picture of Dr Oliver and Mr Peirce examining patients, meant that he was never short of commissions. He portrayed all the most celebrated characters associated with eighteenth-century Bath, including Beau Nash, Christopher Anstey and Ralph Allen. William Pitt, who was in Bath receiving treatment for gout, was delighted with Hoare's portrait of him and wrote that it was 'the very best thing he has yet done, in point of likeness'.

Nash commissioned from Hoare a set of pastels of 'Beauties of the age', but it was among the visitors that his pastels were most popular. Like miniatures, they were cheaper than oil paintings because they were quicker to produce, requiring only two or three sittings. The technique was also one that was enjoying a vogue with amateurs.

ABOVE *A family group painted by William Hoare. The long weeks spent in Bath were often a perfect opportunity to sit for a portrait. Visitors were invited to visit some of the artists' painting rooms.*

Wright of Derby decided to try his luck in Bath but did not have the immediate success of Gainsborough or Hoare, as he described in a letter to his brother:

I have now past one season, the biggest of the two, without any advantage. The Duchess of Cumberland is the only sitter I have had and her order for a full length dwindled to a head only, which has cost me so much anxiety, that I would rather have been without it; the great people are so

fantastical and whining, they create a world of trouble . . .
I am confident I have some enemies in this place, who
propagate a report that I paint fire-places admirably, but
that they never heard of my painting portraits . . . There is
a scheme of some artists here . . . to work me out, and
certainly it proves at present very injurious to me, and I
know not whether it will be worth my while (considering
how little business is done here these four or five years
past) to stay to confute 'em.

Eventually business picked up and, a few months later, Wright was
able to send his brother a slightly more optimistic report, for he
had been commissioned to paint the historian Catherine
Macaulay and her admirer Dr Wilson.

More popular and more prosperous than any of the painters
was Thomas Barker — 'Barker of Bath'. A member of a family
of artists, he came as a young man to Bath, where his talents
impressed Charles Spackman, a rich coach-builder and patron of
the arts. Spackman paid for him to go to Rome to study

BELOW *While the
elderly husband is being
recorded for posterity,
his young wife seeks
solace in the arms of an
admirer, Plate VI from*
The Comforts of
Bath *by Rowlandson.
'Or to PAINTER'S
we repair/Meet Sir
Peregrine HATCHET
there.' Anstey*

painting and on his return Barker set up in Bath. Here, as well as painting portraits, he specialized in local views that were obviously influenced by his knowledge of paintings of the Roman *campagna*. His landscapes appealed enormously to the increasingly romantic and sentimental taste of connoisseurs with money to spend during their stay in Bath.

Unlike the other artists, Thomas Rowlandson came to Bath less in pursuit of subjects and patrons than to assuage his passion for gambling. Heavy losses had a beneficial effect upon his art, compelling him to draw more and more caricatures in order to settle his debts. Rowlandson's twelve *Comforts of Bath* illustrate in comic detail all the events of a day at Bath: drinking the waters in the Pump Room, bathing in the King's Bath, dancing at a ball in the Assembly Rooms and breakfasting in public, as well as a scene at the fish market, a doctor's surgery and portrait artists at work in their studios. Although giving a caricaturist's impression of the pursuit of pleasure, Rowlandson drawings give some idea of the gaiety and the amusements described in Anstey's panegyric on eighteenth-century Bath:

> Of all the gay Places the World can afford,
> By Gentle and Simple for Pastime ador'd,
> Fine Balls, and fine Concerts, fine Buildings, and Springs,
> Fine Walks, and fine Views, and a Thousand fine Things,
> Not to mention the sweet Situation and Air,
> What Place, my dear Mother, with *Bath* can compare?

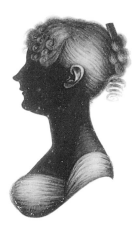

Jane Austen's Bath

JANE AUSTEN'S NAME has for many generations been more or less synonymous with the city of Bath, but as it happened she spent no more than five years of her life here. Her own records of her association with the place lie almost exclusively in the pages of two of her novels, *Persuasion* and *Northanger Abbey* – both published after she died in 1817 – and in the letters written to her elder sister Cassandra.

No letters survive from her first visit, as the guest of a wealthy uncle and aunt, the Leigh-Perrots. That was in 1797, the year Nelson was in Bath recuperating from the loss of his arm in the battle off Tenerife. Her second visit was two years later, when she stayed in Queen Square with her mother and brother Edward, who was taking the cure.

In 1801, when she was twenty-five, and already the author of three successful novels, Jane was taken to Bath for an extended stay, much against her will and for somewhat unexplained family reasons. Her first impressions of the place this time were not enthusiastic, partly on account of having had to leave her much loved home at Steventon and partly, perhaps, because her feelings were tinged with the mortifying fear that her mother was in search of a husband for her.

Mr Austen had arranged, without waiting to consult any other member of the family, to retire from his living at Steventon in Hampshire. His daughters came home one afternoon to be met by their mother. ' "Well, girls," ' she said, ' "it is all settled, we have decided to leave Steventon and go to Bath." ' It is reported that Jane fainted dead away.

THE SEARCH FOR LODGINGS

Upon her arrival in May 1801 Jane wrote from Paragon Buildings to Cassandra, 'from my *own* room up two pairs of stairs, with everything very comfortable about me':

> The first view of Bath in fine weather does not answer my expectations; I think I see more distinctly thro' rain. The sun was behind everything, and the appearance of the place from the top of Kingsdown was all vapour, shadow, smoke and confusion . . . When my uncle went to take his second glass of water I walked with him, and in our morning's circuit we looked at two houses in Green Park Buildings, one of which pleased me very well . . . The only doubt is about the dampness of the office, of which there were symptoms.

The same note of complaint is apparent in another letter, written a few months later:

> To make long sentences upon unpleasant subjects is very odious, and I shall therefore get rid of the one now

ABOVE A general view of Bath from the Claverton Road, from Bath, Illustrated by a Series of Views. *In* Northanger Abbey, *'Miss Tilney, to whom all the commonly frequented environs were familiar, spoke of them in terms that made her [Catherine Morland] all eagerness to know them too.'*

uppermost in my thoughts as soon as possible. –
Our views on Green Park Buildings seem all
at an end; the observation of the damps still
remaining in the offices of an house which
has been only vacated a week, with reports
of discontented families and putrid fevers,
has given the *coup de grace*.

At the start of their time in Bath the Austens were,
it seems, constantly on the move, searching for the
perfect lodgings. This gave Jane an excellent
opportunity to furnish Cassandra with sour descriptions:

> I went with my mother to help look at some houses in
> New King Street, towards which she felt some kind of
> inclination, but their size has now satisfied her. They were
> smaller than I expected to find them. One in particular out
> of the two was quite monstrously little; the best of the
> sitting-rooms not so large as the little parlour at Steventon,
> and the second room in every floor about capacious
> enough to admit a very small single bed. We are to have a
> tiny party here to-night. I hate tiny parties, they force one
> into constant exertion.

Their search ended with an advertisement in the *Bath Chronicle*:

> The lease of No 4. Sydney Place, three years and a quarter
> of which are unexpired at Midsummer. The situation is
> desirable, the Rent very low, and the Landlord is bound
> by Contract to paint the first two floors this summer. A
> Premium will therefore be expected.

It was in the quiet, eastern part of the city, opposite the recently
built Sydney Hotel and public gardens.

Bath, towards the end of the eighteenth century, had begun to
attract a different type of visitor. With its fine streets, concerts and
plays, and a supply of new faces, life was pleasant – and it was
cheap – making it an ideal place for respectable retirement.

Little though she liked the move, Jane did not allow her dismay
to weaken her resolve to find amusement in her new surroundings.

ANNE ELLIOT'S BATH FROM *PERSUASION*
In *Persuasion*, written in 1816, Jane Austen drew heavily upon her
time there, describing the city's life with her own incomparable

ABOVE TOP *The
account rendered for an
advertisement for a house
in Lansdown Crescent
submitted by the printer
of the* Bath Chronicle,
*Richard Cruttwell. It
was in the* Chronicle
*that the Austens saw
an advertisement for
the house they took
in Sydney Place.*

ABOVE *A Bath
lodging-house lady,
her hat the object of
ridicule but her services
indispenable to visitors.*

irony at the same time as allowing the reader to learn of her reluctant presence there through the voice of her long-suffering heroine, Anne Elliot: 'She disliked Bath, and did not think it agreed with her; and Bath was to be her home.'

Anne's first impressions were very much the same as those of the creator of the character. She 'persisted in a very determined, though very silent, disinclination for Bath; caught the first dim view of the extensive buildings, smoking in rain, without any wish of seeing them better'. By no means did Anne share the enthusiasm of her friend, Lady Russell, for 'the dash of other carriages, the heavy rumble of carts and drays, the bawling of newsmen, muffin-men, and milkmen, and the ceaseless clink of pattens'. Anne's father, Sir Walter Elliot, when finding himself financially embarrassed, had, in spite of his foolishness, shrewdly chosen to live in Bath. 'It was a much safer place for a gentleman in his predicament; he might there be important at comparatively little expense.' It also gave him ample opportunity to flaunt his social and physical superiority:

> The worst of Bath was the number of its plain women. He did not mean to say that there were no pretty women, but the number of plain ones was out of all proportion. He had frequently observed, as he walked, that one handsome face would be followed by thirty, or five-and-thirty frights; and once, as he had stood in a shop in Bond Street, he had counted eighty-seven women go by, one after another,

BELOW An engraving looking towards the Sydney Hotel, opposite Sydney Place where the Austens lodged in 1801. Jane was delighted with the position of the house, close to the public gardens. 'We might go into the labyrinth every day,' she wrote.

ABOVE *A concert, Plate
II from* The Comforts
of Bath. *Rowlandson's
print seems to illustrate
Jane Austen's remark,
after a visit to one of
Venanzio Rauzzini's
concerts, that it 'was very
full and very hot'.*

without there being a tolerable face among them. It had
been a frosty morning, to be sure, a sharp frost, which
hardly one woman in a thousand could stand the test of.
But still, there certainly were a dreadful multitude of ugly
women in Bath; and as for the men! They were infinitely
worse. Such scarecrows as the streets were full of! It was
evident how little the women were used to the sight of
anything tolerable, by the effect which a man of decent
appearance produced.

It is to *Persuasion* that we owe much of our knowledge of the
pettiness and intricacy of Bath society at the beginning of the
nineteenth century, and so craftily did Jane Austen mingle the real
with the fictional that it is often hard to disentangle the two.
When Anne Elliot arrived there, her silly father and unsympa-
thetic sister were already at home in Camden Place, 'a lofty
dignified situation, such as becomes a man of consequence'. She
was taken aback to find them so fully embroiled in the minutiae
of the place:

> It was all Bath. They had the pleasure of assuring her that
> Bath more than answered their expectations in every
> respect. Their house was undoubtedly the best in Camden
> Place, their drawing-rooms had many decided advantages
> over all the others which they had either seen or heard of,
> and the superiority was not less in the style of the fitting-up
> or the taste of the furniture. Their acquaintance was
> exceedingly sought after. Everybody was wanting to visit

BELOW AND BELOW
LEFT *Two visitors to
Bath observed by the
watercolourist John
Nixon. In Sir Walter
Elliot's opinion there
were many ugly people
in Bath.*

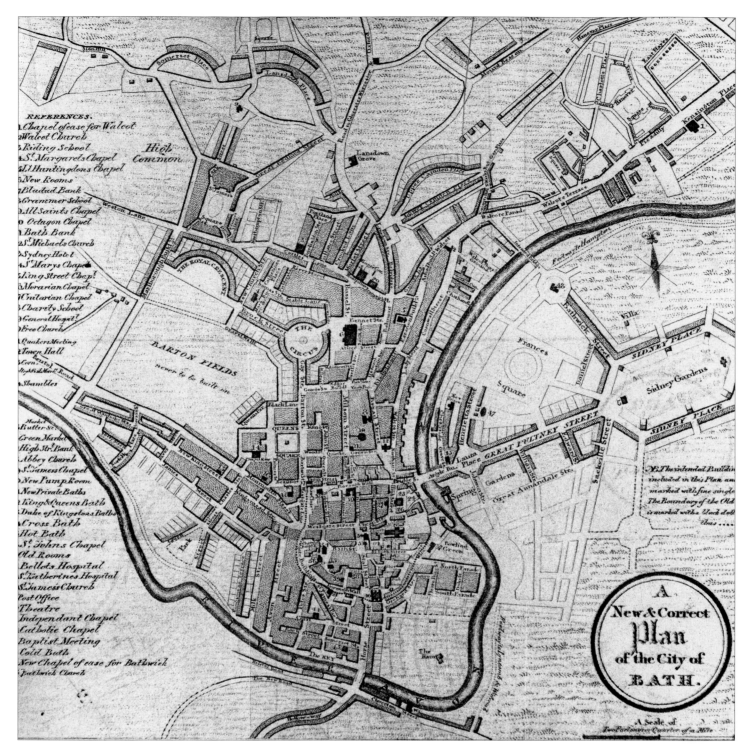

A
New & Correct
Plan
of the City of
BATH.

them. They had drawn back from many introductions, and still were perpetually having cards left by people of whom they knew nothing.

Anne Elliot led her readers into a less comfortable part of the city when she introduced an old school friend, a Mrs Smith, residing in reduced circumstances in lodgings near the hot baths, 'living in a very humble way, unable even to afford herself the comfort of a servant, and of course almost excluded from society'. Jane much

ABOVE *'A New and Correct Plan of the City of Bath', which folded out from* The Original Bath Guide, *1811. This provided essential information for all the visitors.*

enjoyed imagining for her readers how the snobbish Sir Walter reacted to his daughter visiting such a low part of town:

> and who is Miss Anne Elliot to be visiting in Westgate Buildings? A Mrs Smith. A widow Mrs Smith; and who was her husband? One of the five thousand Mr Smiths whose names are to be met with everywhere. And what is her attraction? That she is old and sickly. Upon my word, Miss Anne Elliot, you have the most extraordinary taste! Everything that revolts other people, low company, paltry rooms, foul air, disgusting associations, are inviting to you.

THE BATH OF *NORTHANGER ABBEY*

In contrast to the tranquil *Persuasion*, where Anne Elliot viewed with anguish the idiocies of her relations in search of good society, *Northanger Abbey* presents an altogether more frivolous study of ridiculous behaviour. The novel was begun in 1798 and was ready for publication in 1803, though not published until fifteen years later.

Jane, when she set to work on the novel, already knew for herself the 'difficulties and dangers' of a six weeks' residence which the innocent, if somewhat fanciful, heroine, Catherine Morland, underwent. When Catherine was tugged through the streets of Bath by her false and aspiring friend, Isabella Thorpe, in pursuit of some uninterested young men they had espied in the Pump Room, the author gave us vivid glimpses of the bustle of the time:

> Half a minute conducted them through the Pump-yard to the archway, opposite Union Passage; but here they were stopped. Everybody acquainted with Bath may remember the difficulties of crossing Cheap Street at this point; it is indeed a street of so impertinent a nature, so unfortunately connected with the great London and Oxford roads, and the principal inn of the city, that a day never passes in which parties of ladies, however important their business, whether in quest of pastry, millinery or even (as in the present case) of young men, are not detained on one side or other by carriages, horsemen, or carts.

ABOVE AND BELOW LEFT Trade cards advertising shops in Bath at the close of the eighteenth and beginning of the nineteenth century. Katherine Plymley recorded in March 1799, 'at Linterns music shop I was told he had at that time two hundred Harpsichords and Piano Fortes hired out & as fast as they were return'd from one family they were wanted by another.'

'This evil had been felt and lamented' by Isabella at least three times a day:

> and she was now fated to feel and lament it once more; for at the very moment of coming opposite to Union Passage, and within view of the two gentlemen who were proceeding through the crowds, and threading the gutters of that interesting alley, they were prevented crossing by the approach of a gig, driven along on bad pavement by a most knowing-looking coachman, with all the vehemence that could most fitly endanger the lives of himself, his companion, and his horse.

The irresistibly facetious hero of the novel, Henry Tilney, introduced to her in the Lower Rooms by the Master of Ceremonies, enjoyed perplexing the unsophisticated Catherine with teasing mockery as he asked her for her impressions of the season:

> 'Do you find Bath as agreeable as when I had the honour of making the inquiry before?'
> 'Yes, quite; more so, indeed.'
> 'More so! Take care, or you will forget to be tired of it at the proper time. You ought to be tired at the end of six weeks.'
> 'I do not think I should be tired, if I were to stay here six months.'
> 'Bath, compared with London, has little variety, and so every body finds out every year. "For six weeks, I allow, Bath is pleasant enough; but beyond *that*, it is the most tiresome place in the world." You would be told so by people of all descriptions, who come regularly every winter, lengthen their six weeks into ten or twelve, and go away at last because they can afford to stay no longer.'

ABOVE *A 'Modern Belle' going past the Circus to the Rooms at Bath, a print by James Gillray published in 1796. It satirizes the fashion for ostrich-feather headdresses.*

Besides teasing her, Tilney led Catherine to pleasing spots. 'They determined on walking round Beechen Cliff, that noble hill, whose beautiful verdure and hanging coppice render it so striking an object from almost every opening in Bath.'

A BATH ASSEMBLY

Although less fashionable than it had been some years before – the smart set preferring Brighton to Bath and sea-bathing to the

ABOVE *Detail
from Plate VIII of
Rowlandson's* The
Comforts of Bath. *At
an assembly, a gallant
pays court to a young
woman (her ageing
husband being some
distance away in a
wheelchair). In the
background are tables
of card-players.*

baths – Jane Austen's own inherited world of the country squires
and clergymen remained loyal to Bath. She, with her keen ear,
observant eye and love of clothes, was able to get a great deal
of fun out of life there, and her letters to Cassandra are richly
entertaining. In May 1801 she wrote:

> In the evening I hope you honoured my toilette and ball with
> a thought; I dressed myself as well as I could, and had all my
> finery much admired at home. By nine o'clock my uncle,
> aunt and I entered the rooms and linked Miss Winstone on to
> us. Before tea it was rather a dull affair; but then the before tea
> did not last long, for there was only one dance, danced by
> four couple. Think of four couple, surrounded by about an
> hundred people, dancing in the Upper Rooms at Bath!

After tea, Jane and her companions cheered up:

> The breaking up of private parties sent some scores more to
> the ball, and tho' it was shockingly and inhumanly thin for
> this place, there were people enough to have made five or
> six very pretty Basingstoke assemblies.

Then came the more startling piece of news:

> I am proud to say that I have a very good eye at an
> adulteress, for tho' repeatedly assured that another in the

same party was the *she*, I fixed upon the right one from the first. A resemblance to Mrs L. was my guide. She is not so pretty as I expected . . . she was highly rouged, and looked rather quietly and contentedly silly than anything else.

MADAME D'ARBLAY AND MRS PIOZZI

In one of Jane's early letters from Bath she mentioned that a bespectacled undergraduate from Oxford, who was of their party, had heard that *Evelina* had been written by Dr Johnson. The author of the novel was, as she knew, Fanny Burney, who in 1793 had married a French émigré, the chevalier d'Arblay. Jane had been among the subscribers to her later, and much less successful, literary venture, *Camilla: Or a Picture of Youth*.

As a young woman Fanny had visited Bath with Mrs Thrale, the friend of Dr Johnson. In 1815 she came with her husband, who had been wounded in the leg by a kick from a horse:

> I wish to live at Bath, wish it devoutly; for at Bath we shall live, or no longer in England. *London* will only do for those who have two houses, and of the *real country* I may say the same . . . Bath, therefore, as it eminently agrees with us all, is, in England, the only place for us, since here, all the year round, there is always town at command, and always the country for prospect, exercise, and delight.

Madame d'Arblay called on Mrs Piozzi, the former Mrs Thrale, who after her first husband's death, and much to the consternation of her friends, had married Gabriel Piozzi, an Italian singer. The most memorable event of Mrs Piozzi's last years, during which she apparently lived in a state of 'rampant senility', was the party she gave in the Assembly Rooms in 1820 to celebrate her seventy-ninth birthday. At the ball that was part of the entertainment, she led the dancing, it was said, with an astonishing display of 'elasticity'.

BONNETS AND NECESSITIES

Jane Austen was inordinately fond of clothes and finery, as she illustrated time and again in her letters to Cassandra:

> My mother has ordered a new bonnet, and so have I; both white strip, trimmed with white ribbon. I find my straw bonnet looking very much like other people's and

BELOW *A. Edouart's silhouette of a gentleman about to enter the Assembly Rooms. In* Northanger Abbey, *the Master of Ceremonies introduced Catherine to 'a very gentleman-like young man as a partner; his name was Tilney'.*

quite as smart. Bonnets of cambric muslin on the plan of Lady Bridges' are a good deal worn, and some of them are very pretty; but I shall defer one of that sort till your arrival. Bath is getting so very empty that I am not afraid of doing too little. Black gauze cloaks are worn as much as anything. I shall write again in a day or two.

And in another letter:

When you have made Martha's bonnet you must make her a cloak of the same materials. They are much worn here in different forms – many of them just like her black silk spencer, with a trimming round the armholes instead of sleeves; – some are long before and some long all round.

The Rev. James Woodforde, who came from very much the same milieu as the Austens, paid almost as much attention as Jane to the intricacies of everyday life, and particularly to prices. When he visited Bath in 1795, and put up at the 'very capital' White Hart Inn in Stall Street, he recorded in his diary paying two shillings for a pair of elastic soles for shoes; three-and-sixpence for a 'Tunbridge Soap Box with Naples Soap'; and two shillings for a small shaving-brush in an ivory case. He tells, too, how, after a long early morning walk, he gave a shilling to a barber for shaving him and dressing his wig.

LEFT *A watercolour by
Fanny Burney's cousin
Edward Francis Burney
of ladies amusing
themselves doing
fancywork.*

JANE'S LAST DAYS IN BATH

The Austen family sojourn in Bath ended in 1805, the year of the
Battle of Trafalgar, and, had it not been for the sad cause, would
have come as a relief to the thirty-year-old Jane. On 21 January
1805 she wrote to her brother, Frank, to tell him the 'melancholy
news' of the death of their father. Bowen, the apothecary, had
visited him, and at the end he had been attended by Dr Gibbs.

Jane's scorn – and probably disappointment – at the people to
be found in Bath was shared at about the same period by a
Frenchman named Simond. 'Bath is a sort of great monastery,
inhabited by single people, particularly by superannuated females,'
he wrote.

The Swedish E. G. Geijer went to a ball in the Assembly
Rooms and found there:

> a multitude of made-up, painted hags' faces, enamelled
> with brand new smirks, figures sinking under the assaults
> of time and under the magnificence of raiment and
> diamonds and pearls.

Jane's observations were rather more personal than these, but then
she had had time to become acquainted with some of the habitués
and knew that they presented more amusement to her than interest:

I cannot anyhow continue to find people agreeable; I respect Mrs Chamberlayne for doing her hair well, but cannot feel a more tender sentiment. Miss Langley is like any other short girl, with a broad nose and wide mouth, fashionable dress and exposed bosom. Adm: Stanhope is a gentlemanlike man, but then his legs are too short, and his tail too long.

In March 1805 Mrs Austen with her daughters moved into lodgings at 25 Gay Street. In spite of the sadness that her father's death caused her, Jane was more than capable of entertaining Cassandra with descriptions of her last days at Bath:

There was a monstrous deal of stupid quizzing, and common-place nonsense talked, but scarcely any wit; – all that border'd on it, or on sense, came from my Cousin George, whom all together I like very well.

RIGHT *The Three Bath Deities, 'Humbug, Follee and Vanitie', the* frontispiece to Bath Characters or Sketches from Life *by Peter Paul Pallet. In a similar vein, a visitor wrote that Bath society was made up of 'broken fortunes, broken constitutions and broken hearts'.*

Wee thre Bath Deities bee: Humbug, Follee, & Vanitee.

The Continuing Story

THE GENTLE AND CIRCUMSCRIBED world in which Jane Austen spent her days was very different from the exotic world of William Beckford. A pale, remote eccentric, Beckford was ostracized by polite society after he was believed to have had a homosexual affair with the young William 'Kitty' Courtenay. In 1796, with the help of the architect James Wyatt, he put up a tower as tall as the spire of Salisbury Cathedral and two wings of his Gothic-inspired Abbey in the grounds of Fonthill, near Tisbury in Wiltshire. It was in some respects the realization of a tower described in his romantic novel *Vathek*. The materials used were so weak, however, that in 1800 the tower fell down in a gale. Undeterred, he rebuilt the tower and lived in the Abbey, surrounded by the remarkable collection of works of art he had put together, until accumulating debts forced him to sell the Abbey as well as most of the collection.

Moving to Bath in 1822, he toyed with the idea of buying Prior Park with the proceeds of the sales but in the end chose to live at No. 21 Lansdown Crescent. Soon afterwards he acquired No. 20, and because the houses were on either side of the entrance to a mews, he built a bridge to link the two. A few years later he added No. 19, to avoid being 'perpetually annoyed by the ticking of some cursed jack, the jingling of some beastly piano, horrid toned bells tinkling, and so on'. It was bought, he said, 'to the infinite annoyance and astonishment of the Bath aristocracy, an odd breed I believe'.

As well as the three houses, Beckford bought all the land behind, right up to the top of Lansdown Hill, and there, between

RIGHT *The interior
of Beckford's belvedere,
decorated in scarlet,
crimson, purple and
gold, from Willes
Maddox's* Views of
Lansdown Tower.

1825 and 1826, he built another tower, as a place of retreat and to house books, manuscripts, furniture and works of art from his original collection. It was designed by the Bath architect Henry Edmund Goodridge in an Italianate style.

When he was young Beckford had inherited a huge fortune from his father, and it was also as a wealthy young man that the writer Walter Savage Landor came to Bath in 1805. He, too, was a figure of some eccentricity. He loved Bath, finding that it had many similarities with Florence, and here, in the Assembly Rooms, he first set eyes on 'the nicest girl in the room' and determined to marry her. And so he did.

One of Landor's visitors at Bath was Charles Dickens, who reproduced some of Landor's peculiarities, not unkindly, in the character of Boythorn in *Bleak House*. On a trip to see the older man, Dickens might have noticed the name Pickwick on the signpost to a village, or the sign of Moses Pickwick, a coach proprietor in Bath.

The morning after his arrival, Mr Pickwick of *The Pickwick Papers* was introduced to the Master of Ceremonies, Angelo Cyrus Bantam, Esquire, M.C., and welcomed to 'Ba-ath'. Bantam was gorgeously attired in a very bright blue coat, black trousers and the thinnest of highly polished boots:

> A gold eye-glass was suspended from his neck by a short broad black ribbon; a gold snuff-box was lightly clasped in his left hand; gold rings innumerable glittered on his fingers; and a large diamond pin set in gold glistened in his shirt frill. He had a gold watch, and a gold curb chain with large gold seals; and he carried a pliant ebony cane with a heavy gold top . . . His features were contracted with a perpetual smile; and his teeth were in such perfect order that it was difficult at a small distance to tell the real ones from the false.

BELOW Entrance to Bath from the Bristol Road by T. H. Shepherd, 1829. Bath was by now a busy city, with an increase in permanent residents adding to the general bustle.

In the evening this figure of ridicule, this imaginary successor to Beau Nash, emerged from his chariot at the door of the Assembly Rooms in even more fanciful dress, though with 'the same teeth, the same eye-glass, the same watch and seal', and, 'if possible, just a thought more scented'. At the ball, 'Dresses rustled, feathers

waved, lights shone, and jewels sparkled'; brilliant eyes lit up with pleasurable expectation.

Mr Pickwick drank the waters in the Pump Room and played whist with three ladies, who were so desperately sharp that they quite frightened him. He let Miss Bolo down so badly as her partner that she 'rose from the table, and went straight home, in floods of tears, and a sedan chair'.

The Pickwick Papers were the posthumous papers of the Pickwick Club of Dickens's invention and described a time a little earlier than their initial appearance in monthly instalments in April 1836. By then a sedan chair of the kind in which Miss Bolo was transported from the Card Room was rarely to be seen in the streets of Bath, having been replaced by the Bath chair. And much else was changing, too. When Queen Victoria came to the throne in 1837, Bath had ceased to be a place of fashionable resort, for it had many rivals, both in England and on the Continent. There were no longer diplomatic reasons to prevent those wishing for a change of

ABOVE AND BELOW LEFT *South Parade in 1828, a watercolour by Robert Woodroffe. In the street is a Bath chair such as the one from the manufacturer's catalogue of Leveson & Sons. The chair had a steering wheel and required only one man to push or pull it.*

air and a change of scenery from crossing the Channel, and the railway had made distant places easier to reach.

There were now almost 30,000 permanent residents, including more than a sprinkling of spinsters, retired clergymen and half-pay officers, whereas in the first part of the eighteenth century there had been no more than 3,000. Victorian terraces were built to house this increase in the permanent population, but they had nothing of the grace and elegance of their Georgian predecessors. The mixed company of Nash's day was disappearing, and life was altogether less fashionable, less amusing. Bath was becoming, in effect, a provincial town like any other.

Thomas Baldwin, in redeveloping the area around the Baths in the 1780s and 1790s, had discovered the Roman Temple of Minerva, and more discoveries of the ancient origins of the city were to come in the following century. In 1864 James Thomas Irving came to Bath as Clerk of Works to Sir Gilbert Scott, who was carrying out some restorations on the Abbey. Irving measured and recorded all his archaeological finds, and a much more detailed picture began to emerge. Then, at the turn of the century, Charles Edward Davis excavated the Roman reservoir, finding the votive offerings already described, and uncovered the Roman

BELOW *A late Victorian postcard of Bath chairs waiting at the door of the Pump Room.*

ABOVE *George Street, Bath, painted by John Christian Maggs in 1879. York House in George Street was the traditional stopping-place for the coaches.*

Great Bath. More exciting finds have been made since, and it has become possible to visualize almost the entire Roman precinct.

At the same time as the archaeological discoveries were being made, there was a growing feeling that the wonders of Georgian Bath should be saved from destruction. This was to lead eventually, in 1934, to the formation of the Bath Preservation Trust. The Trust played a part in ensuring that the damage done by wartime air raids was properly repaired, and has fought with the utmost tenacity to prevent or limit destructive modernization of the city.

In 1968 No. 1 Royal Crescent, a lodging house in a bad state, was bought by Major Bernard Cayzer and given to the Bath Preservation Trust, whose headquarters it became. After an authentic job of restoration and refurbishment, it opened to the public in 1970 as an example of an eighteenth-century town house. Only materials available at that period were used, and great attention was paid to the detail. It complements the careful re-creation of the Georgian era carried out for The Royal Crescent hotel, at No. 15 and No. 16.

Let us remember Bath in its Georgian heyday as it was ecstatically discovered by Smollett's Lydia Melford:

> Bath is to me a new world. All is gaiety, good-humour, and diversion. The eye is continually entertained with the splendour of dress and equipage; and the ear with the sound of coaches, chaises, chairs, and other carriages. The merry bells ring round from morn till night.

And let us conclude on a gentler, more reflective, note with lines from Algernon Swinburne's 'Ballad of Bath':

> City lulled asleep by the chime of passing years,
> Sweeter smiles thy rest than the radiance round thy peers;
> Only love and lovely remembrance here have place.
> Time on thee lies lighter than music on men's ears;
> Dawn and noon and sunset are one before thy face.

ABOVE *The Pump Room in 1884, painted by James Lamont Brodie. Dickens's Mr Pickwick, who was lodged in the Royal Crescent, drank a regular half pint in the Pump Room, 'tasting of warm flat irons'. Visitors can still drink the water here today.*

PLACES TO VISIT

The ballroom

ASSEMBLY ROOMS
Bennett Street, Bath.
Tel. 01225 477789;
Fax 01225 428184

The Assembly Rooms, built by John Wood the Younger and opened in 1771, were at the centre of the social life of Bath in the late eighteenth and early nineteenth centuries. They were known then as the New or Upper Rooms, to distinguish them from the two earlier Assembly Rooms, which do not survive. The building comprises a large ballroom, the Octagon, which was the card room until a new one was added, and a tea room. Balls and subscription concerts were regular features of the season. The Rooms were puchased by the Society for the Protection of Ancient Buildings in 1931 and, through the generosity of Ernest Cook, given to the National Trust. They suffered severe bomb damage in 1942. After successive phases of reconstruction and restoration, the Rooms were reopened in their present form in 1991, with colour schemes based on the historical evidence.

BATH ABBEY HERITAGE VAULTS
Tel. 01225 422462

Restored eighteenth-century cellars beside the south side of Bath Abbey house an exhibition relating the story of Christianity on the Abbey site since the Roman period. Archaeological remains give pointers to early Saxon and Norman building, and then to the Abbey's Tudor revival and Victorian restoration. In addition there are vignettes of the Abbey's position during the Civil War and among eighteenth-century visitors.

BECKFORD'S TOWER, BATH
Lansdown, Bath. Tel. 01225 338727

An extraordinary tower house with a unique stone spiral staircase built for William Beckford in 1827 by the architect H. E. Goodridge. It has fine views over the city of Bath and is surrounded by a wilderness garden. Beckford used it as a retreat and to house his collection of precious objets de vertu, *paintings and rare books.*

THE BUILDING OF BATH MUSEUM
The Countess of Huntingdon's Chapel,
The Vineyards, The Paragon, Bath.
Tel. 01225 333895

The eighteenth-century 'gothick' chapel built by the Countess of Huntingdon is the setting for a museum that chronicles the development of Georgian Bath. Detailed displays and models show how the city was

Fragments of eighteenth-century wallpaper

Holburne Museum

designed, built, decorated and lived in. They include architects' plans and explanations of the quarrying and working of Bath stone, joinery, plasterwork decoration, and the original paints and wallpapers.

HOLBURNE OF MENSTRIE MUSEUM AND CRAFTS STUDY CENTRE

Great Pulteney Street, Bath.
Tel. 01225 466669; Fax 01225 333121

The museum is housed in the former Sydney Hotel, surrounded by the Sydney Pleasure Gardens, which were much frequented by late eighteenth-century and Regency residents and visitors. The nucleus of the collection was formed by Sir William Holburne, a noted nineteenth-century collector who lived in Bath. It includes Old Master paintings, bronzes, maiolica, porcelain, glass, furniture, portrait miniatures and silver, as well as pieces that relate to the history of the city. The Crafts Study Centre has a permanent collection of work by important twentieth-century British artist-craftsmen on view: ceramics, textiles, furniture and woodwork, and calligraphy.

MUSEUM OF COSTUME

Assembly Rooms, Bennett Street, Bath.
Tel. 01225 477789; Fax 01225 444793

Displays in a part of the Assembly Rooms show the changing styles of dress for men, women and children from the late sixteenth century to the present day. The collection, one of the largest and finest in Britain, was formed by the designer, collector and historian Doris Langley Moore and given by her to the city of Bath in 1963. It includes examples of the richly embroidered men's suits and brocaded silk dresses worn by fashionable society in the Georgian period.

NO. 1 ROYAL CRESCENT

1 Royal Crescent, Bath.
Tel. 01225 428126

The first house of John Wood the Younger's famous crescent, rescued, restored and furnished by the Bath Preservation Trust to give an authentic impression of an eighteenth-century town house.

OCTAGON GALLERIES

Royal Photographic Society, Milsom Street, Bath.
Tel. 01225 462841; Fax 01225 448688

The Octagon Chapel, built in 1789, is the head-quarters of the Royal Photographic Society and its important collection of historic and modern photographs. The gallery has changing exhibitions of photographic work, some from its own collection and some showing new work.

PUMP ROOM

Abbey Churchyard, Bath.
Tel. 01225 477000

This, the second Pump Room to be built, overlooks the King's Bath and dates from 1795. The spa water may still be drunk (at no cost to disabled visitors and Bath residents). On view are the famous clock presented by its maker, Thomas Tompion, to the city of Bath in 1709 and the marble statue of Beau Nash, which was placed in the first Pump Room in 1752. Original artefacts on display include sedan and Bath chairs.

POSTAL MUSEUM
8 Broad Street, Bath.
Tel. 01225 460333

The first known posting of the world's first stamp, the Penny Black, took place from this historic building on 2 May 1840. Displays introduce the history of letter writing, and how the mail was carried, including the story of the pioneering Bath Mail Coach.

PRIOR PARK LANDSCAPE GARDEN
Tel. 01225 833422

Eighteenth-century landscape garden set in a valley overlooking Bath, created by Ralph Allen with the help of the poet Alexander Pope and the landscape gardener Lancelot 'Capability' Brown. The house is a school (and not open to the public) but the garden, run by the National Trust, still has many of its original features: the Palladian Bridge, grotto, Rock gate, Sham bridge, Wilderness and Serpentine lake as well as remnants of the cascades.

Prior Park

Roman mosaic

ROMAN BATHS MUSEUM
Abbey Churchyard, Bath.
Tel. 01225 477785

The great steaming Bath, with some stones unmoved since the Roman period, together with the remains of the magnificent Roman temple, are the principal features of the museum. In addition, many of the finds made over the last 300 years, illustrating the history and archaeology of the Roman Baths and the city, are on display. The exhibits include sculpture, coins and jewellery.

VICTORIA ART GALLERY

Bridge Street, Bath.
Tel. 01225 477772

The gallery puts on view a selection from the city's permanent collection of British and European art from the seventeenth century to the present day. Represented are works by artists who worked in Bath, including William Hoare, Gainsborough and Thomas Barker. Works from the fine collection of watercolours are also displayed, some of which illustrate everyday life in Bath.

WILLIAM HERSCHEL MUSEUM

19 New King Street, Bath.
Tel. 01225 311342

A typical Georgian terrace house, built in 1766, which was the home of the musician, composer and astronomer William Herschel and his sister Caroline. It was from the back garden of this house, looking through a seven-foot telescope he had constructed himself, that in 1781 he discovered the planet Uranus. Exhibits include items relating to the Herschel family: musical instruments and concert programmes, optical mirrors, lenses and telescopes, and letters and documents concerning Herschel's work. Also on view is the workshop where he set up his furnace and lathe.

Herschel Museum

Note on the Bath Preservation Trust

Beckford's Tower, The Building of Bath Museum, Herschel House and Museum and No. 1 Royal Crescent all come under the aegis of the Bath Preservation Trust, which works for the preservation and improvement of Bath's architecture and environment. As well as managing the museums, the Trust is involved in conservation on a small scale, including the restoration of original stonework, railings, exterior lamps, fanlights and glazing bars. All such architectural details are well worth noting on a tour of the city. Anyone interested in the work of the Trust should contact it at No. 1 Royal Crescent, Tel. 01225 428126.

BIBLIOGRAPHY

ANSTEY, CHRISTOPHER: *The New Bath Guide*,
5th ed., London, 1767

BARBEAU, A: *Life and Letters at Bath in the XVIIIth
Century*, London, 1904

Bath History, vols 1–5, Bath, 1986-94

CRUIKSHANK, DAN, AND BURTON, NEIL: *Life in the
Georgian City*, London, 1990

CUNLIFFE, BARRY: *English Heritage Book of Roman
Bath*, London, 1995

EARLE, JOHN: *Bath Ancient and Modern*, London
and Bath, 1864

FAWCETT, TREVOR: *Voices of Eighteenth-century Bath*,
Bath, 1995

GADD, DAVID: *Georgian Summer*, Bath, 1971

GOLDSMITH, OLIVER: *The Life of Richard Nash*,
London, 1762

HINDE, THOMAS: *Tales from the Pump Room*,
London, 1988

ISON, WALTER: *The Georgian Buildings of Bath*,
London, 1948

LOWNDES, WILLIAM: *The Royal Crescent in Bath*,
Bristol, 1981
The Theatre Royal at Bath, Bristol, 1981

LEES-MILNE, JAMES, AND FORD, DAVID: *Images of
Bath*, Richmond-upon-Thames, 1982

MELVILLE, LEWIS: *Bath under Beau Nash*, London, 1907

MORRISS, RICHARD: *The Buildings of Bath*,
Stroud, 1993

MOWL, TIM, AND EARNSHAW, BRIAN: *John Wood:
Architect of Obsession*, Bath, 1988,

PENROSE, REV. JOHN: *Letters from Bath*, 1766-1767 ed.
B. Mitchell and H. Penrose, Gloucester, 1983

ROBERTSON, CHARLES: *Bath, An Architectural Guide*,
London, 1975

ROLLS, ROGER: *The Hospital of the Nation*, Bath, 1988

SMITH, R. A. L: *Bath*, London, 1944

SMOLLETT, TOBIAS: *Humphry Clinker*, ed. J. P. Brown,
London, 1872

WOOD, JOHN: *An Essay Towards a Description of Bath*,
3rd ed., London, 1765

INDEX

ACKNOWLEDGEMENTS

AUTHOR'S ACKNOWLEDGEMENTS

Thanks are due first and foremost to Elizabeth Drury and Philippa Lewis, who have been much more than editor and picture researcher. I am grateful to those involved with The Royal Crescent hotel, the architect William Bertram, who gave me a copy of his thesis on Queen Square and shared an enthusiasm for John Wood, and the decorator Rupert Lord, who has such a feel for the eighteenth century. Dan Cruikshank gave me permission to make use of his work on Queen Square in *Life in the Georgian City*, which he wrote with Neil Burton; the latter, who is Secretary of the Georgian Group, made helpful comments on the chapter 'The Building of Georgian Bath'. A debt is owed to Tim Mowl and Brian Earnshaw for their research into the building of the Circus, published in their fascinating work *John Wood Architect of Obsession*. Finally, thanks are due to John Lewis and John Tham for their support and encouragement.

PICTURE ACKNOWLEDGEMENTS

The illustrations in this book are published by kind permission of the following:

Amoret Tanner Ephemera Collection 1, 134, 145, 148, 149; Bath Archaeological Trust 10, 17 (photos Tim Mercer) 13, 14, 15, 154; Bath Central Library 85, 108, 133, 137 Bath Preservation Trust: The Building of Bath Museum 62, 64, 65, 152 (Joseph Self Collection); Beckford's Tower 144, 146; William Herschel Museum 123,155; Bridgeman Art Library 19, 40, 52, 89, 109, 130, 131, 132, 141; British Library 18, 33, 42, 49, 58 left, 84, 98, 101; British Museum 29, 124; Mike Caldwell 12 top, 21, 60; Christie's Images 51, 115, 142; James Crathorne 20, 25; Edifice Photo Library 56 bottom, 58 right, 63, 71 bottom, 153; Holburne Museum & Crafts Study Centre, Bath 45, 88, 93, 103, 122, 140; National Portrait Gallery 70; National Trust at Cliveden (photo Cliveden hotel) 55; National Trust Picture Library 152, 154; Private Collection 96; R.I.B.A. British Architectural Library Drawings Collection 22; Roman Baths Museum & Pump Room 11, 50; Royal Academy of Arts, London 16; The Royal Crescent 6, 61, 75, 78, 79, 80, 81, 82 (photos Mike Caldwell); 44, 54, 94, 95, 104, 111, 113, 114, 119, 133 bottom, 135 top, 138, 139, 143, 150, 151; Royal National Hospital for Rheumatic Diseases 24, 26, 28, 31, 36, 37, 38 (photos Clive Quinnell); Kim Sayer 48 right, 74; Sotheby's Picture Library, Private Collection 127; Victoria & Albert Museum, London 53; Victoria Art Gallery, Bath 8, 56 top, 106, 110, 118, 121 (Museum photos), 2, 34, 39, 57, 66, 68, 71, 72, 87, 92, 99, 100, 102, 116, 125, 128, 135 bottom (photos Bridgeman Art Library); 30, 32, 47, 48 top, 69, 97, 120, 147, 148, (photos Courtauld Institute of Art); Wellcome Centre Medical Photographic Library 35; Yale Center for British Art, Paul Mellon Collection 105.

The illustration on the endpapers is *The South East Prospect of the City of Bath* by Samuel and Nathaniel Buck, 1734 (Bath Central Library)
FRONT COVER: Royal Crescent (photo John Heseltine)
BACK COVER: The Royal Crescent hotel balloon (photo Mike Caldwell)

The author and publishers would also like to thank the following for their help in the preparation of this book: Ross Stevenson General Manager at The Royal Crescent, Fiona Hills at Fotek and Gillian Sladen.